Managing Resources for Improvement

Educational management series

Series editor: Cyril Poster

Managing Resources for School Improvement

Creating a Cost-Effective School

Hywel Thomas and Jane Martin

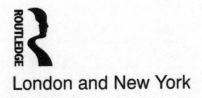

London and New York

First published 1996
by Routledge
11 New Fetter Lane, London EC4P 4EE

Simultaneously published in the USA and Canada
by Routledge
29 West 35th Street, New York, NY 10001

Typeset in Palatino by
Ponting–Green Publishing Services, Chesham, Bucks
Printed and bound in Great Britain by
Clays Ltd, St Ives PLC

British Library Cataloguing in Publication Data
A catalogue record for this book is available from the
British Library

Library of Congress Cataloguing in Publication Data
A catalogue record for this book has been requested

ISBN 0–415–12910–9

Contents

Tables

Preface

How are secondary schools using their greater responsibilities over resources and how are their decisions on resources linked to the standard and quality of learning? In this book the experience of 18 locally managed and grant maintained secondary schools is described and we show how resources have been used to support new developments and initiatives. We also examine how decisions were made and, above all, we consider their effect on the experience of pupils.

The schools were selected as examples of good practice and provide an opportunity to learn from the potential and benefits of delegating responsibilities for resource management to the school site. Their experience is interpreted by drawing upon an analysis of the attributes we associate with the cost-effective school. This analysis not only provides a means for interpreting the experience of these 18 schools but also a means by which others can review their own approach to resource management and consider how it can be improved. In this way, the book is not only designed to inform the day-to-day practice of governing bodies, head teachers and teachers but offers a new and distinctive theoretical analysis of decentralised resource management.

Acknowledgements

We should like to thank: all who responded to our requests for information; the head teachers, all staff and governors in the schools who facilitated so carefully the work of the reasearch team; the parents and pupils who responded to the questionnaires; the Chair and members of the DFE Steering Group for their advice and support; Dr Alison Bullock, the University of Birmingham, for her advice, comment and assistance; Jane Cheng for her assistance in data processing; and computing, secretarial and reprographics staff at the University of Birmingham.

Part I

Linking resources to improvement

Chapter 1

Resources and improvement

Resources matter. Those who work in schools as teachers and associate staff, school premises, furniture, books and equipment all provide some of the means by which we transform our hopes and aspirations for children's education into daily learning opportunities and experiences and, beyond that, into the longer-term outcomes of schooling. It is that link between resources and learning which is the principal concern of this book. We ask what characteristics would be expected in a school that is successful in making the link between resources and learning – the cost-effective school – and then examine how 18 secondary schools exercised their responsibilities for resource management.

The importance of resources for schools is highlighted by debate about the government's annual decisions on public expenditure on education and its consequences for spending by schools. It is a debate which manifests genuine concern about the level of spending on education and it is a concern we share. This book, however, is not about that debate but what is, in many ways, the more challenging task of whether we use existing resources as effectively as we might. Difficulties in articulating the link between resource decisions and learning are a general problem, as identified in the annual report of Her Majesty's Chief Inspector of Schools:

> Inspectors judged the *evaluation of cost-effectiveness* by governors and head teachers unfavourably in nearly two-thirds of the primary and nearly half of secondary schools. Few of the primary schools had, for example, procedures to monitor the effectiveness of their deployment of support staff; and while awareness about cost-effectiveness is increasing in secondary schools, few schools evaluate the cost of their procedures and plans .... Many schools require more rigorous methods for assessing the costs and opportunity costs of alternative plans.
>
> (Ofsted, 1995, p.24)

On this assessment, there is clearly scope for improvement in the way we manage resources in schools and, in so doing, improve the quality of experiences provided. This book, based upon a study originally commissioned by the DFE as part of a wider international project co-ordinated by the Paris-based OECD, is about how schools can improve upon their management of resources.

We examine and report on resource management in 18 secondary schools originally selected as possible exemplars of good practice, their selection followed consultation with the regional offices of HMI in England. Thirteen of the schools are under local management (LMS) and five are grant maintained (GMS), so that we represent the two main forms of decentralised resource management in maintained schools in England and Wales. Drawing upon a combination of survey data and case studies, the study examined evidence related to three key questions:

- How are these secondary schools using their greater responsibilities over educational resources?
- What are the characteristics of the decision-making processes which relate resources to learning?
- How is the exercise of these responsibilities linked to the standard and quality of learning in the schools?

We show how these 18 schools have used their responsibilities over resources to undertake and support initiatives and developments in the schools. We examine how the decisions were made and how these relate to the wider context of decision making in the schools. Above all, we consider the effect of these changes on the experience of pupils in the schools.

In drawing upon the practice of resource management in schools, the book has been written for a wide audience. It is intended to be useful for governors and head teachers with the responsibility of ensuring that they are using their budgetary resources to best effect. We anticipate that the content will also be useful for inspectors and for the monitoring and support role of LEA officers. As an empirical report on radical forms of decentralised resource management the text should also be of interest to readers in those many countries embarking on policies decentralising resource management to the school level. Finally, we anticipate that it will be a useful book for students in the UK and elsewhere engaged in short and long courses in educational management.

This is a wide range of audiences and we anticipate that the book will fulfil different needs for each of them; accordingly, we set out below eight features of the book that will be of interest to the different audiences.

A DISTINCTIVE CONTRIBUTION

First, the book provides an opportunity to learn from *good practice* in secondary schools in a wide range of settings. The schools which we contacted were identified following discussions with HMI and LEAs, drawing upon their local knowledge across the regions of England, and following preliminary contacts by ourselves. The choice of good practice schools merits emphasis. We make no claim that this book provides a basis for generalising about decentralised management in England and Wales, an issue examined in *Schools at the Centre?* by Alison Bullock and Hywel Thomas (1996). We would claim, however, that this examination of good practice provides valuable insights into the practice of decentralised management in different settings.

Second, we believe that the framework used for organising our research work has potential for guiding resource management in schools. The framework introduced in Chapter 3 has been used and well received by a wide range of audiences during training sessions on school management and development planning. We have now extended this framework so that it provides a statement of the attributes of a cost-effective school. In subsequent chapters, this extended framework is used to interpret the evidence collected from schools and is used to provide guidance on the practice of resource management.

Third, we consider how the link between resources and learning can be improved. While these schools were selected on the basis that they represented good practice in resource management, we do not suggest that we consistently observed best practice. It is clear that there is potential for further development in how they exercised their new responsibilities. The changes we examine are recent and all schools are still learning how best to manage in these conditions. The evidence from the schools indicates weaknesses which can be improved upon and we consider how this might be done.

Fourth, the 18 schools include a range of types serving a diversity of communities and, in the Appendix, we provide a brief description of each school. They include 11–16 and 11–18 schools ranging from 607 to 1,765 pupils, mixed and single sex, inner city and rural. There are schools with a large proportion of pupils from ethnic minorities, others with an intake from predominantly white low income communities and yet others serving middle income communities. Seventeen of the schools were comprehensive and one selective. They were drawn from across England, a feature we were able to retain in the three schools selected for more detailed case study.

Fifth, we believe this to be the first major study of resource management which has included and compared the two main forms of decentralised resource management in England and Wales: the local management of schools (LMS) and grant maintained schools (GMS). The number of each type, 13 LM and five GM, are not proportionate to their number but fewer than five GMS seemed too few to include in a study of this kind. In undertaking our work, we asked much the same questions and used the same approaches in collecting data. The result contributes to a distinctive

understanding of the differences and similarities between these two forms
of decentralised management. It has also contributed to our views on how
decentralisation might be developed.

Sixth, the study is distinctive in its collection of information from a wide
range of people with direct interests in the schools. We interviewed and
surveyed governors, head teachers and teachers, a range of support staff,
parents and pupils. We also observed meetings of governors, faculties and
departments, as well meetings of senior staff. It provides an unusually
wide range of voices and opinions on resource management and its
contribution to school improvement. In the first phase of the study,
we conducted over 100 interviews. In the three case study schools we
conducted more than 70 interviews, attended 26 meetings and collected
survey opinions from over 300 parents of Year 9 pupils and over 500 Year
9 pupils.

Seventh, the study provided an opportunity to examine how head
teachers – notably in the three case study schools – interpret their roles in
this area. We report not only on a diversity of styles but on an interpretation of role that was sensitive to context, notably the state of development
of their school. We consider the similarities and diversity in the interpretation of the head teacher's role in these schools and go on to examine the
implications for the professional development of head teachers.

Finally, we draw upon the study as a whole for a discussion of its
implications for the internal management of schools and of the wider
school system. Our purpose is to consider how changes can contribute to
assuring quality in schools and make recommendations on the role of
governors, head teachers, LEAs and the DFEE. While located in the context
of the LMS and GMS of England and Wales, our conclusions are linked to
the conceptual analysis of the cost-effective school and, therefore, are
relevant to the development of decentralised systems elsewhere.

Taken together, we believe these eight factors offer insights into decentralised resource management for the several audiences we have mentioned. How we have organised the remainder of the text is set out in the
following section.

THE STRUCTURE OF THE BOOK

The book contains eight further chapters organised in three main parts.
Part I is called 'Linking resources to improvement' and contains two
context-setting chapters. Chapter 2 examines the main features of locally
managed schools (LMS) and grant maintained schools (GMS). By identifying those elements which are common and those which differ, the
emphasis is upon providing an understanding of those aspects of the
changes which relate to the management of resources. Such an approach
may be of particular interest to students of resource management as

well as to readers outside England and Wales less familiar with these changes.

How resources are linked to the quality of provision and to school improvement is the theme of Chapter 3. It draws upon relevant literature and proposes a framework which is used both to examine the schools in this study and to provide guidance for readers seeking ways of improving their own practice in the management of resources. It begins with a diagram intended to provide a visual expression of the link between resources and learning and is accompanied by an examination of the linkages between resources and the activities which support learning. This provides a basis for an extended analysis of the organisational attributes of cost-effective schools, by which we mean schools using their additional responsibilities over resources (costs) in ways that are educationally successful (effective). Taking account of the practice of development planning in schools, the analysis considers the pervasive uncertainty in school management, the distinction between delegation and autonomy, the nature and extent of dialogue over educational needs and the quality of data informing those dialogues. The analysis concludes with a statement of the organisational attributes we would expect to see in a cost-effective school, a specification upon which we draw in the remainder of the book.

The second part of the book is titled 'Resourcing improvement in practice' and draws on the data collected from the 18 secondary schools in our study. In Chapter 4 we report on the wide range of ways in which the schools have used their responsibility over resources. We also examine the decision-making processes linked to these choices and assessments of their effect on the experience on pupils. This is followed by chapters on the three schools selected for more detailed case studies. At the end of each chapter we review the evidence using our 'model' of the cost-effective school.

Broome School is a locally managed school in the centre of a large city and has a very high proportion of pupils from ethnic minority populations. The case study provides an account of the resource choices of the school and its decision-making processes. It includes information on decision making within departments and reports on how pupils and parents assess the changes, as well as their views of the school as a whole. The case study examines how the management and leadership of the head teacher takes account of the circumstances of the school and the experience of its staff.

Skelton School is a large comprehensive school on the suburban edge of a conurbation in the north east of England. The case study has similarities with that of Broome in that it examines choices, the decision-making processes and the assessments of parents and pupils. In its reporting, however, it describes and analyses the different nature of the head teacher's leadership and considers this issue in the context of his length of service and the experience of the staff.

In Chapter 7 we report on Whittaker School, a large comprehensive in a town in a rural area close to a large conurbation. It is a grant maintained school. As with the other case studies, the choices made with resources, the decision-making processes and assessments of effects on pupils are all reported. The leadership of the recently appointed head teacher is examined and how her role has taken account of the specific circumstances of the school is considered.

The final part of the book is titled 'Securing improvement'. In Chapter 8, we consider the ways and means by which improvement is assessed in schools. In drawing upon the data from the study we review the ways in which those interviewed describe the effects of changes on the learning experiences of pupils. This includes an examination of differences in perspectives among the different groups from whom information was collected – governors, head teachers and senior staff, teachers, support staff, parents, pupils and students. We review what this means for managing improvement and being or becoming a cost-effective school.

In Chapter 9 we examine what has been learnt from this study on ways and means by which schools can use their greater responsibilities over resources for managing improvement. This will consider a number of themes. It will examine the sensitivity of leadership styles to the specific contexts of schools and how this needs to be taken into account by head teachers as they begin working in a new school. We ask whether the existing forms of delegation are appropriate for all head teachers and all schools and what changes might be introduced. The chapter discusses lessons for systems of communication and the importance of forms of staff development, particularly those which ask challenging questions about existing patterns in the deployment of resources in schools. There will also be attention given to the key issue of feedback on quality, inviting schools and government (local and national) to consider the ways in which they inform themselves and others about what is taking place in schools and in classrooms. We present this as a particular and fundamental challenge to those with responsibility for the management of schools and their duty to use those responsibilities to secure improvement in classroom practice and the achievement of learners.

CONCLUSION

We recognise that resources alone are no guarantee of the quality of teaching and learning or of the nature and standard of longer term outcomes. Much depends upon the commitment of pupils and the support of their parents and community. Indeed, any assessment of how well schools are doing – the debate on learning value added – must take account of these factors. Much does depend, nonetheless, upon how schools use and manage those resources that are under their control. In examining and learning from the practice of the schools in this study, our concern is to assist in improving upon the existing practice of resource management. On the basis of the comments of HM Chief Inspector cited earlier, this would not be before time.

Chapter 2

Reforming resource management

Reviewing more than a decade of its reforms to schools in England and Wales, the Department for Education (DFE) in 1992 identified 'five great themes' embodied in the changes:

> Five great themes run through the story of educational change in England and Wales since 1979: quality, diversity, increasing parental choice, greater autonomy for schools and greater accountability.
>
> (DFE/WO, 1992, p.2)

As might be expected, these themes are evident in the legislation of this period and, in the first main section of this chapter, it is upon that legislation that we draw to provide an account of the national context in which our study is located. It is within that context that the subsequent two sections examine specific aspects of change in resource management and their implications for school improvement. A fourth section draws attention to different ways of providing 'greater autonomy for schools'. It is an important element in an argument which calls for sensitivity in understanding national and international differences in delegated management.

A PROGRAMME OF CHANGE

The Conservative government elected in 1979 was committed to wide-ranging reforms, of which education was one part. In education, the first legislative expression was the 1980 Education Act which included changes relevant to what were later identified as the 'great themes' of diversity, choice and accountability. Diversity and choice were encouraged by ending further moves towards non-selective secondary education and by creating a scheme which financed access to schools in the private sector, 'enabling pupils who might not otherwise be able to do to benefit from education at independent schools' (Section 17). Accountability was addressed by changes to the governance of schools. The Act provided that, in general, all schools should have individual governing bodies and it was made a requirement that membership must include elected parent governors and elected teacher governors. The constitution and functions of governing bodies were set out in Instruments and Articles of Government and model articles which dated back to 1944. These gave governing bodies duties in relation to the care of school premises, budgeting and the appointment and dismissal of staff. In practice, however, the exercise of these powers varied widely across England and Wales and, at that time, few schools exercised any significant power with respect to finance.

The 1986 Education Act addressed the themes of accountability and autonomy through further changes to the membership and responsibilities of governing bodies. The Act strengthened the framework of accountability by prescribing the number and membership of governors. For example, for *county* schools with over 600 pupils, the governing body will have 19 members, five of whom are parents, five from the maintaining Local Education Authority (LEA), two teacher governors, the head teacher if he or she chooses and a further six governors who represent various interests outside the school. Within this last group are co-opted governors who provide a means by which the governing body must ensure that they have links with the business community. This is an illustrative example and does not cover all schools of this size. For example, there are *aided* and *special agreement* schools where the majority of governors are nominated by a foundation body, normally the Church. Here also, the Act specifies the composition of the governing body. The Act provided that the conduct of the school is under the general direction of the governors, except where specific functions are assigned to others. In terms of enhancing the accountability of schools, these functions included a requirement to prepare an Annual Report for Parents and a duty to hold an Annual Meeting of Parents to discuss the report and the running of the school generally. The accountability of the LEA to the school was increased by requiring the LEA to give a governing body an annual statement of the cost of running the school, covering day-by-day and capital expenditure. Changes in procedures for the appointment and dismissal of staff gave more control to schools, an important step in increasing their autonomy in the selection of staff. The autonomy of schools was further increased by giving governing bodies greater control of the use of premises outside school hours.

All five 'great themes' can be identified in the wide-ranging 1988 Education Reform Act. The Act introduced a statutory National Curriculum and arrangements for national assessments of all pupils. By defining the curriculum which it required schools to provide for pupils of 5 to 16 years, it could be argued that the government declared its view on 'quality'. In effect, the National Curriculum and the related Programmes of Study and Statements of Attainment can be viewed as a declaration about the expectations which the government has for the standard and quality of education of children attending the nation's schools, other than those in the independent sector. The arrangements for national assessment also reflected the government's concern with the theme of 'accountability' since it is a means by which the government ensures that parents, public and government obtain more information about the performance of schools.

The 1988 Act also introduced a system of school management known as the local management of schools (LMS). The 1988 Act extended the powers of governing bodies so that they took control from the LEAs of the larger part of their expenditure, and are given almost complete responsibility for the appointment and dismissal of staff. LMS gives schools 'autonomy' but they are held accountable for their management by the publication of examination results, the provision of information on the national assessments and through reporting at the Annual Parents' Meetings.

The themes of 'diversity' and 'parental choice' are embodied in the introduction of grant maintained schools (GMS) and City Technology Colleges (CTCs). These institutions are not part of LEAs. GMS own their land and buildings and are the employers of staff. GM schools have control over all their funding and are responsible for the provision of almost all services for the pupils and students at their school. Limited exceptions to this responsibility relate to the continuing statutory responsibility of LEAs for the statementing of pupils with special educational needs. GM schools not only have greater autonomy than locally managed schools but are seen by the government as a means of providing a greater diversity of schools, enabling the government to extend parental choice. This theme is also taken into account by a change in the admission arrangements of most schools – LMS and GMS – so that they are required to admit pupils to the physical capacity of the building.

Legislation since 1988 has continued to apply the five themes to which we have referred. The School Teachers' Pay and Conditions Act, 1991 put in place the means by which the Secretary of State for Education can pursue policies which provide for more flexibility and autonomy over pay at the level of the school and the individual teacher. The 1992 Education (Schools) Act altered procedures for the inspection of schools so that the accountability of schools is more public. From September 1993, all schools entered a cycle where they can expect to be inspected once every four years using a framework devised by a national Office for Standards in Education (Ofsted). The results of these inspections are published, not least to inform parents about the performance of schools.

The 1993 Education Act includes changes in the procedures for assessing the requirements of children with special educational needs. It also defines a framework for managing an education system where many schools are grant maintained and no longer part of Local Education Authorities.

Recent changes, therefore, no less than those of more than a decade ago, can be interpreted within the themes with which we began this chapter and which were identified by the government in 1992. What is also apparent, however, is the coherence of these changes and their relationship with the theme of resource management and school improvement which is the focus of this book. In examining this coherence we begin with an analysis of reform as management provided by Sir John Caines, a recent Permanent Secretary at the (then) Department of Education and Science (DES).

REFORM AS MANAGEMENT

'The 1988 Act', according to Sir John Caines, 'was not just about change and managing change. It was also about changing the way in which the delivery of education was to be managed' (Caines, 1992, p.15). By management, he means:

> setting realistic goals and drawing up plans to achieve them. Those plans involve distinct phases: setting objectives, allocating resources, delivering results, evaluating the impact, resetting objectives in the light of evaluation.
>
> (p.16)

His account notes that management is an activity which takes place at all levels and includes schools and teachers, LEAs and the DES. It can be applied to different facets of change. Thus, he writes of the way the National Curriculum has required schools to plan its implementation and to consider the curriculum across the school as a whole. This, he suggests, has led to greater teacher participation in whole school planning. He also recognises that teachers and schools have had to adapt their plans as a result of changes in national policy, circumstances which at least show 'that the Government has been prepared to make changes in the light of schools' experience' (p.18), a comment received with some irony by those attending the lecture. Implicit in his account – made explicit in a question and answer session at the conference and attended by one of the authors of this book – is the place of the government in setting strategic national objectives for the curriculum. The management role of the government is to set the framework and the Programmes of Study for the curriculum while allowing schools to work out how best to implement these changes within the timescale set down for them. The distinctive role of schools in these respects was argued by Michael Marland (1991) who draws attention to that part of the 1988 Act which 'contains a firm denial of the Secretary of State's right to control anything other than the definition of the National Curriculum components'. Section 4, Subsection 3 states that:

> An order made under Section 2 may not require –

(a) that any particular period or periods of time should be allocated during any key stage to the teaching of any matter, skill or process forming part of it; or

(b) that provision of any particular kind should be made in school timetables for the periods to be allocated to such teaching during any such stage

For these and other reasons, Marland (1992) concludes that, in determining their curriculum, schools need to be aware that each aspect of the National Curriculum has to be incorporated, but it is schools who decide when, how and in which context. He argues that the powers of head teachers and governors over the curriculum are legally well founded and considerable: it is not 'the DES or the Secretary of State (who) are controlling the totality, shape, style or delivery pattern of a school curriculum. The school is the centre of curriculum planning' (p.19), a view which is congruent with Caines' own analysis of the nature of management.

Consistent with this analysis is the delegation to schools of greater control over financial resources. This gives schools the opportunity to allocate resources to meet needs. Here also, however, the government can be seen to be setting the strategic objectives. The delegation of financial authority to schools has been done within a national framework which requires, for example, 80 per cent of the money allocated by a funding formula to be tied to pupil numbers. It means that schools get money according to rules which are designed to encourage competition, so that those schools which are popular with parents receive additional funds as their enrolment rises. In important respects, therefore, changes in curriculum and in the management of resources are wholly consistent with Caines' analysis of the management changes of the 1988 Act: national frameworks with some scope for local decision on implementation.

While this account may be a persuasive statement of the new management of education, it is not sufficient for understanding its rationale. This requires some account of the direction of change. With respect to the curriculum, for example, the setting of a national framework took away from schools an autonomy over the curriculum which was a distinctive feature of the system in England and Wales. The decentralisation of control over resources, on the other hand, granted an autonomy which schools previously lacked.

While this apparent paradox of control and autonomy can be explained in terms of an analysis developed from Caines' discussion of management, it does not provide a framework for understanding the rationale for change. Simkins (1992, pp.7–8) analyses the shift to managerial control as a restructuring of the accountability of professionals:

The argument here is that professional autonomy and judgement must be subordinated to broader 'corporate' purposes. This cannot be achieved by the 'collegial' methods of shared responsibility favoured by professionals – such methods are often more rhetoric than reality anyway. It is necessary to establish clear organisational goals, agree means for achieving them, monitor progress, and then support the whole process by a suitable system of incentives. Only in this way can it be ensured that the organisation is effective in the accomplishment of its goals and efficient in its use of resources.

He goes on to consider alternative ways of developing systems for accomplishing managerial control of professionals, suggesting arrangements which vary in their emphasis upon hierarchic control as against incentive systems. The precise form of autonomy over resources represents such an incentive system, the emphasis upon competition ensuring that autonomy is exercised in ways which are intended to be sensitive to the needs and perceptions of parents.

What may occur in practice, of course, may be altogether more complex and akin to a 'mixed economy' of management (Thomas, 1994). Consider the perspective of head teachers in this new context. They must work at bridging the tension between a prescribed National Curriculum and the need to secure 'ownership' of that curriculum by teachers. Faced with pressures to compete, heads must emphasise the quality of their schools – in terms of resources, processes and outcomes – while, in other professional contexts, they may wish to voice concern about the level of resources provided for education. In working within and between each of these different contexts, heads as managers have to appeal to different facets of human motivation: by turn encouraging, persuading, cajoling, negotiating and commanding. Life within schools calls upon all of these motives: the skilful educational leader appeals as appropriate to the blend which is relevant to a particular circumstance.

In these respects the educational leader may be little different from leaders in any organisation, working within a 'mixed economy' of management, using appropriate techniques for the achievement of ends. Whether education and its management is in some way special, however, is a theme to which we shall return following later chapters in this book. What is clear, in any event, is that management is a central theme of reform and relates closely to this study. How it links resources to improvement is the focus of the next section, which examines in greater detail the LMS and GMS components of the 1988 Education Reform Act.

RESOURCES AND IMPROVEMENT

Decentralised management, crucially located within a strategic national framework, is central to achieving the government's 'five great themes' of contemporary reforms. This becomes apparent when we examine six components of decentralisation: financial delegation, formula funding, changes in admission arrangements, staffing delegation, performance indicators and choice of governance. The discussion has been organised to allow the reader to observe the inter-relationship of these parts and the common elements of the two main forms of delegated management: locally managed schools and grant maintained schools.

The first component of decentralisation is *financial delegation*, giving schools autonomy with respect to day-to-day control over their budgets. It is the national extension of practices which were developed in the 1980s in Cambridgeshire (Downes, 1988) and Solihull (Thomas, 1987) where schools were allowed to move money from one item of budget to another. Based on the premise that schools make better decisions than LEAs when identifying resource priorities, it is a change in management processes intended to make more effective use of those resources. It means, for example, that within their cash limited budgets, schools decide on the numbers and type of staff and how to spend money on their premises.

The second component of decentralisation is *formula funding*, introduced in April 1990. It has transformed the practice of funding schools from one characterised by a lack of information on the level of funding of individual schools to a system where the rules of funding are transparent with the funding of individual schools open to public scrutiny. This means that, in the same LEA, schools which are comparable in type and pupil intake are funded on the same basis, meeting an equity condition which did not necessarily obtain before 1990. The formula is also a pupil-driven system of funding schools in which a minimum of 80 per cent of the money allocated by formula must be tied to a pupil so that 'schools have a clear incentive to attract and retain pupils' (DES, 1987). This has some similarities to an education voucher. It gives the exercise of parental choice a financial impact because, effectively, the money follows the pupils. This also contributes to accountability through the automatic nature of punishment or reward for schools viewed as unsuccessful or successful. The interaction of this change with the other elements of decentralisation makes it a much more significant change than the financial delegation initiatives of Cambridgeshire and Solihull.

If we link the formula to the changes in *admission arrangements* we see emerging a system which enables parents to move children to more popular schools, knowing that much of the money follows the child. The change on enrolment policy is at once modest and potentially significant. The 1988 Act ended the powers of LEAs and governing bodies to cite 'efficiency' arguments for imposing admissions limits below the capacity of a school. In future, schools – other than selective and church schools – must admit pupils to their physical capacity. This change clearly refers to the theme of parental choice and accountability. It has been further developed by an announcement in 1992 that all secondary schools can now admit up to 15 per cent of their intake according to certain curriculum criteria, provided these do not involve selection in terms of academic subjects.

Now tie the formula and the enrolment change to the fourth component of *staffing delegation*. This gives governors powers of appointment, suspension and dismissal over the teaching and non-teaching staff based at the school. It allows schools to choose staff suitable to their needs – autonomy – but it also requires schools which are losing pupils to nominate staff for redundancy – accountability. Pupil-driven funding, admitting pupils to the capacity of schools and making staffing levels dependent on the size of the school's budget combine into pressure upon schools to compete so that, in the government's analysis, improved performance – quality – is secured.

These near-market aspects of decentralisation are given further emphasis with the development and use of more *performance information* about schools. Parents need data on school performance if they are to make choices and the range of data now published is a part of this process, typically provided in a prospectus distributed to prospective parents. Data already available or becoming available include examinations results, performance on the national assessments linked to the National Curriculum, rates of pupil attendance and levels of unauthorised absence. Governing bodies are also required to report on their expenditure of the school budget. Further information is made available as the inspection procedures generate reports on individual schools.

Parents can also exercise choice over *school governance* since it is through a ballot of parents that schools can proceed with an application to become grant maintained (GM). As the numbers of grant maintained schools increase, so does the diversity of schools available to parents. We have noted in this chapter and earlier, that GM status gives schools direct funding from the DFE and is intended to finance all the services provided for pupils. The governing body is the employer of staff at the school, owns the land and buildings, is responsible for their upkeep and development and is the body responsible for pupil admissions. In May 1995, the number of GM secondary schools in England was 630, about 17 per cent of the total of about 3,750 secondary schools.

These six components of decentralisation have a coherence, each supporting the others and contributing to the themes of 'quality, diversity, increasing parental choice, greater autonomy and accountability'. What is also notable, however, is that they are free-standing changes: each could have been introduced without the others. While the six do form an integrated package, therefore, each can be examined separately and that has been our intention in this study.

Our principal focus is on financial and staffing delegation, examining how schools have used their enhanced authority in these areas to secure improvement. To the extent that we also examine the consequences of different forms of governance, as represented by the locally managed and grant maintained schools in our study, it is through the prisms of financial delegation and staffing delegation. We do not, for example, examine the implications of the altered composition of governing bodies, the consequences of new procedures for admission of pupils or the changes in relationships between the schools and central and local government. That it is possible to identify different components of decentralisation, and examine them separately, alerts us to the final theme of this opening discussion.

THE LIMITS OF COMPARISON

It is apparent that LMS and GMS differ significantly in the extent of their responsibilities over resources. Both also differ in the extent of their responsibilities from the schools in the Cambridgeshire and Solihull resource management initiatives of the 1980s. Yet, the words *delegation, decentralisation* and *autonomy* have variously been used to describe all of these distinct forms of resource management with too little recognition of significant policy and organisational differences. The scope for confusion can be illustrated by the government's decision to adopt the term *self-governing schools* to describe GMS, a phrase similar to the *self managing school* coined by by Caldwell and Spinks (1988) as a generic description for different forms of decentralised school management.

These comments are intended as a warning against comparisons which treat the language of decentralisation and delegation as unproblematic. In different countries these words can carry meanings which are the opposite of usage in England and Wales. For example, in a recent comparative study of the 'movement to transform and control performance of schools', Koppich and Guthrie (1993) refer to site-based management in the USA as one in which 'essential educational decisions, including budgeting, personnel selection, and *curriculum* [emphasis added], devolve to the school site' (p.58). Even where decentralisation initiatives are similar to those in England and Wales, as in New Zealand (Macpherson, 1993), the retention by the central authorities of the power to appoint and dismiss school staff marks a substantial difference with decentralisation in England and Wales where staffing delegation is a key component.

CONCLUSION

In this chapter, we have set out the nature and context of educational change in England and Wales. We have argued the primacy of certain conceptions of management in understanding the change, and the place of management in making the link between the use of resources and school improvement. Subsequently, we have defined the limits of our own investigation and warned of the dangers of oversimplified international comparisons, more especially if they are undertaken without an analytical framework which is sensitive to differences as well as similarities.

The changes we have described and discussed are substantial, creating new and distinct circumstances for schools. Indeed, so novel are they that there may be limits to what we can learn from previous forms of resource management. Whether this is so will become apparent following a review of the relevant literature on resource management and school improvement.

Chapter 3

The cost-effective school

The future is an uncertain place. Yet, decisions we make daily – great and small – are about that future. Any head teacher making budget proposals for the forthcoming year, for example, cannot know how events will unfold and what will be their implications for actual expenditure. In making those decisions, however, anxieties are tempered by experience, which tells us – and head teachers – that the coming year may not be too dissimilar from present circumstances, of which we are more certain. Or are we? What if the present is also an uncertain place, of which we not only know too little but where some circumstances may not be knowable? There are no guidelines from research and practice, for example, on the effects of spending different proportions of the school budget on teachers as against support staff. Will it ever be possible to advise a school that it is spending the right amount on books, as against other learning resources? Even if it is conceivable that research could answer these questions in the future, for the present we must recognise that much of our decision making occurs in conditions of uncertainty – about the nature of the present as well as the future. Recognition of uncertainty stands in marked contrast to the certainties implied in some definitions of management, such as that of Caines' cited earlier: 'setting objectives, allocating resources, delivering results, evaluating the impact' (op. cit.) all have the ring of certitude.

We begin with these observations as uncertainty provides a key component for the analysis in this chapter, the purpose of which is to explore an answer to a question more easily asked than answered: *how do we recognise a cost-effective school?* In seeking an answer, our intentions are theoretical and practical. Theoretically, a conceptual framework defining the cost-effective school is a means by which we can attempt an assessment of whether schools are using their additional responsibilities over resources (costs) in ways that are educationally successful (effective); and such a framework provides a guide for undertaking an evaluation of the performance of our 18 schools. For practice, developing answers to a question on how we recognise cost-effective schools can provide insights for those with day-to-day responsibility for their management and for the preparation of suitable programmes of professional development.

In setting out to specify some of the characteristics of cost-effective schools, we are embarking upon a novel task. We recognise the requirement placed upon school inspectors in England and Wales to make judgements about efficiency, effectiveness and value for money, part of the family of concepts in which cost-effectiveness is located, but we are aware of difficulties encountered in making reliable and consistent judgements; an examination of 66 secondary school inspection reports by Levacic and Glover (1994, p.25) concluded:

> Our analysis suggests that there is a tendency to use the term efficiency when systems and processes are under consideration. The phrase is likely to be mentioned in commentary on the planning process, or the allocation of resources, and the achievement of some sort of balance between the possible deployment of financial and human resources. The term effective appears to be used, as it should, in relationship to the achievement of outcomes, more often it relates more to processes as in the description of departmental practice . . . . Frequently, however, there is either interchangeability or parallel use of the terms . . .

> The concept and criteria for the judgement of value for money appear also to be lacking precision and are subject to variable usage. In the main it appears to be a judgement about educational outputs, given the environmental context, relative to unit cost. However, in some cases the inspectors' assessment of efficiency in relation to management processes appears to be the dominant criterion. The lack of sufficiently clear guidance on the application of the value for money criteria leads to inconsistencies in the summative comments and, in these early inspections, to avoidance of making a value for money judgement at all.

Hopefully, through its consideration of cost-effectiveness analysis to school settings, this chapter may clarify the use of efficiency-related concepts in appraising school performance. In doing so, we develop a framework for guiding our study and analysis, but our conclusions remain tentative and we look to further studies and theoretical work in this field. The framework is situation specific, developed for application to the delegation of resource management as introduced in England and Wales. Any scope for application and adaptation to other settings must take account of their legislative and cultural contexts.

We begin, appropriately, by defining what it is we mean by cost-effectiveness in this context, recognising that its application to an understanding of the impact of delegated resource management on school performance differs from other applications of the concept. This is followed by a section which draws upon writing on delegated management, school effectiveness and school improvement. The first part examines evidence on the impact of delegated management in England and Wales, whilst the second draws upon theoretical and empirical work on how delegation might best be managed. This informs the following section, which considers what might be the distinctive characteristics of schools which are effective in harnessing resources to learning – *the cost-effective school*. It provides a framework for the remainder of the book, informing the approach we took to the collection and analysis of data and our concluding discussion. The final main section explains how this framework informed our study.

RESOURCE MANAGEMENT AND COST-EFFECTIVENESS

Words like 'cost-effectiveness' and 'efficiency' are among the more abused words from the lexicon of economics, not least because they have often been used by UK governments in the last decade and more as a code for cheapness. It is not our usage and it is, moreover, a usage which is contrary to their meaning within economics. Indeed, far from harming the quality of educational activity, cost-effectiveness analysis can provide an approach for enhancing quality. Properly applied, cost-effectiveness analysis in schools is concerned with the relationship between the learning of children and the human and physical resources which contribute to that learning. It is not concerned with parsimony or cheapness and is not limited to financial outlays but to the use of financial and other resources, assessed in relation to the educational outcomes sought by the school.

As a concept and in its application, *cost-effectiveness* is at once wider and more challenging than *effectiveness*, although the concepts are well matched. An earlier study notes the distinction:

> effective schools are those in which pupils of all abilities achieve to their full potential. Whether that performance is achieved using more rather than fewer resources is not, strictly, a part of the assessment of effectiveness. On the other hand, the amount of resources is an essential component of the assessment of cost-effectiveness. Thus, if two schools which are comparable in every respect are equally effective in terms of performance, the one that uses the smaller amount of resources is the more cost-effective. A school that uses its resources more cost-effectively, moreover, releases resources which can be used to promote further development. Cost-effectiveness, in this sense of the term, is highly desirable.
>
> (Mortimore and Mortimore with Thomas, 1994, pp.20–1)

In addition to its relationship with effectiveness, cost-effectiveness is related to the concept of efficiency and, by examining that relationship, the importance of uncertainty in our analysis becomes more apparent.

Economic efficiency

> refers to the use of the budget in such a way that, given relative prices, the most productive combination of resources is used. That is, no alternative combination of resources, given the budgetary constraint, would enable the organization to produce a higher output.
>
> > (Levin, 1976, p.153)

Production possibilities are assumed to be

> governed by certain technical relationships, and the production function simply describes the maximum output feasible with different sets of inputs ... it represents the maximum achievable output for given inputs.
>
> > (Hanushek, 1979, p.353)

On this criterion, we can be confident that schools are not efficient. This is partly a consequence of imperfections in the labour market so that labour and other factors are not easily substituted for each other, as a result of which price does not represent what economists call marginal productivity. There is an added difficulty that schools are multi-purpose organisations and the achievement of some goals is not always compatible with others. Above all, however, our statement that schools are not efficient turns on the absence of a convincing or wholly adequate *predictive* theory of learning, and such a theory is a prerequisite for specifying clear technical relationships as a basis for the relationship between inputs and educational outcomes. In other words, since we do not *know*, in any final or objective sense, precisely how pupils learn and the appropriate mix of resources to support that learning, we cannot expect schools to meet the demanding technical conditions required by the concept of efficiency. By the same token, of course, we must be careful not to claim too much about our knowledge of the attributes of the effective school. While much can be learned from studies of the factors contributing to effectiveness, they do not tell us whether schools are as effective as they might be.

At best, therefore, schools can seek to be cost-effective rather than efficient; it is an efficiency-related concept but is not predicated upon the same demanding technical conditions. Cost-effectiveness is concerned with comparing different ways of achieving the same objective and the most cost-effective choice will be the least costly of alternatives being compared. For the reasons cited above, this will not necessarily be efficient.

Cost-effectiveness analysis can be applied to schools in a variety of ways. The dominant methodology emphasises quantitative techniques, where predominantly financial resources are measured and related to quantitative indicators of educational outcomes, often scores on scholastic achievement tests. Windham and Chapman (1990) provide a useful discussion of this approach and Behrman (1993), in a paper which reflects both the dominance of work by US scholars and its application in the evaluation of World Bank programmes, a critical analysis of many studies. A range of 12 possible approaches are identified by Thomas (1990, pp.57–8), however, in a discussion of the assumptions underlying the concepts of costs and effectiveness. It is a chapter which notes the dominance of one approach and the influence of about three other methodological perspectives but comments that 'in practice, research studies undertaken on costs or effectiveness often do not fit their paradigm perfectly' (p.57).

Our purpose, however, is not to identify an approach to undertaking a specific *exercise* in cost-effectiveness analysis but to identify the general *organisational characteristics* associated with schools that are effective in appraising their use of resources in relation to their educational purposes. This requires us to have a conceptual framework which recognises costs and effectiveness but also demands a wider organisational context. It is for this reason that we now turn to the literature on delegated resource management, school effectiveness and school improvement. An account of the initial impact of delegated management is followed by a discussion of empirical and theoretical literature on how these responsibilities might best be managed within schools.

DELEGATION, EFFECTIVENESS AND IMPROVEMENT

The impact of delegation

Schools have always managed resources. In the sense that governing bodies, head teachers and teachers have discretion over the use of their time, the management of resources is nothing new for schools in England and Wales. With respect to direct control of money, however, delegation and discretion was much more modest. Typically, it has been restricted to the purchase of books and other learning resources and amounted to about 3 per cent of their budget. LMS and GMS are, however, quite different. For the first time, schools in England and Wales are allowed to decide on the whole pattern of spending on their delegated budget. Under LMS and GMS, governing bodies and head teachers have the 'freedom to take expenditure decisions which match their own priorities' (DES, 1987). The *financial delegation* and *staffing delegation* represented by these freedoms owe much to schemes of delegation developed by a small number of Local Education Authorities in the early 1980s. Accounts from those who participated in and researched those schemes provide some of the evidence on the effect of delegation.

Financial delegation in Solihull was premised on the view that 'if schools were given the right to spend their budget, as though the money was their own, it would be spent in a way which was more carefully attuned to their needs than if the decisions were made elsewhere' (Humphrey and Thomas, 1985, p.419). Accounts based upon visits to schools in Solihull and interviews with head teachers and teachers certainly bear out a belief in its benefits for the school (Thomas with Kirkpatrick and Nicholson, 1989, Chapter 2, *passim*). Further support for this view is given by published accounts from head teachers in the Authority (Hewlett, 1988; Kirkpatrick, 1988). This was also the assessment made in a report commissioned by the government to advise on how schools and LEAs should prepare for LMS: 'there can be major gains from delegation . . . it will give schools the flexibility to respond directly and promptly to the needs of the school and its students in a way which will increase the effectiveness and quality of the services provided' (Coopers and Lybrand, 1988, p.7). These are themes which can be cited also from accounts of financial delegation in Cambridgeshire (Downes, 1988) and from influential accounts of other forms of delegation elsewhere (Caldwell and Spinks, 1988).

An enthusiasm for delegation is no less evident with the introduction of LMS and GMS. A study for the National Association of Head Teachers (NAHT) on the impact of local management on 800 primary and secondary schools shows head teachers as welcoming delegation with few wishing to return to previous arrangements (Arnott, Bullock and Thomas, 1992). A welcome for delegated budgets was also apparent in the 63 schools which informed an HMI report in 1992: 'Most schools with delegated budgets welcome their control over finance and the greater flexibility over purchasing services' (DFE, 1992, p.11). HMI also reported that 'the first observable effect of LMS has been improvement in the premises' and that 'The management focus is being sharpened and staff are participating more fully in forward planning'. A study by Marren and Levacic (1992) on the first year of LMS in 11 schools confirms its popularity but comments that the degree of budget constraint was an important factor in the ability of schools 'to plan their resource use in relation to identified priorities'. For some schools, this meant pursuing the implementation of a number of objectives stated in the development plan but for others it meant the shelving of priorities and decisions where 'educational considerations have had to give way to financial considerations (pp.146–7).

Positive attitudes to delegation also emerge from reports on grant maintained schools. A report by HMI drawing upon 81 GMS, mainly secondary, found that 'They are adapting well to the new framework within which they operate and are taking advantage of the opportunities open to them'. It observed that 'Morale has risen in step with improvements in resources, accommodation and management' (Ofsted, 1993, p.2). A study by Bush *et al.* (1993) reported 80 per cent of the participants in their research claiming independence from the LEA as one of the main benefits of GMS: 'Freedom, financial freedom and a feeling that we are in control of our own destiny' (p.200).

Affirmations of enthusiasm for LMS or GMS are important in them-selves and contribute to our understanding of the change. In themselves, however, they tell us little about the consequence of delegation for the standard and quality of learning. The fundamental test of delegation must be in terms of its effect on pupils in schools which, as Levacic observes: 'is the $64,000 question to which diametrically opposing answers are hotly but speculatively debated' (1992, p.27). She is right to identify 'proponents' of LMS who claim that it contributes to improved effectiveness but she is equally right to resist an easy judgement on this.

The survey of over 800 locally managed schools by Arnott, Bullock and Thomas (1992) asked head teachers to respond to a number of statements on the impact of delegation on the learning of students. It showed head teachers quite evenly divided in their assessment of whether or not 'pupils' learning is benefiting from LM'. The final report on the same study contained longitudinal data which followed a smaller group of schools and these showed heads becoming more positive in their assessment. For the 117 primary schools who responded to the statement in each year, 30 per cent agreed in 1991, 44 per cent in 1992 and 47 per cent in 1993. Among the 40 secondary schools who completed the statement in each year, 34 per cent agreed in 1991, 46 per cent in 1992 and 50 per cent in 1993 (Bullock and Thomas, 1994). Differences in assessing benefits are not unrelated to evidence on funding. The responses to the statement that 'learning is benefiting' correlated with responses to the statement 'I can show a number of increases in provision as a result of LM'. Those head teachers who agreed with this last statement were far more likely to agree with the statement that learning is benefiting. To a significant extent it appears that the assessment of the effect upon learning depends upon heads being able to identify increases in provision, whether these are a result of the new funding arrangements, greater levels of delegation or growth in pupil numbers.

While these studies suggest that delegation is welcomed by schools, therefore, they cannot be regarded as a guarantee of greater effectiveness. Clearly, at the level of public reporting, delegated resource management has been a great success *and it would be unwise too hastily to discount these assessments of the benefits of delegation*. Yet, it is the job of researchers to be sceptical and to keep asking for convincing evidence of success, and the bench-mark of that must be what happens to pupils and students. Reports from school inspections provide some of this evidence. HMI's assessment of locally managed schools reported:

There is little evidence yet of LMS having any substantial impact on educational standards, although specific initiatives have led to improve-ments in the targeting of resources and staff, and so to improvements in the quality of educational experiences.

(DFE, 1992, p.11)

A report by HMI on GMS examined standards of students' achievements and the quality of teaching and learning. Although it stressed the problems of making comparisons it sought, nonetheless, to do so. On standards, 'in 3 per cent more of the lessons [in GM schools] the standards were judged to be satisfactory or better' but no differences were statistically significant. On quality of teaching and learning, however, the percentage of lessons which were satisfactory or better, and good or very good, were more favourable than in non-grant-maintained schools inspected over the same period (Ofsted, 1993, p.10). An investigation of 70 GM schools undertaken by the National Audit Office examined financial management, purchasing and estate management and external audit (National Audit Office, 1994). The report on financial management includes comments on decision making and planning, observing that while 'strategic planning is good at some schools, such planning is generally in its infancy' (p.12). It goes on to advise that development plans should include the financial implications of proposals and include 'detailed objectives and targets for different activities within the school', although examples of performance measures are limited to attendance figures and exam results.

That it is difficult to establish clearly the effect of LMS and GMS on standards and quality should not be surprising. They have been introduced at the same time as other substantial changes in schools, and distinguishing the effect of one from others is inevitably difficult. In parallel with delegation, schools have been introducing the National Curriculum and have been required to prepare Development Plans. Differentiating the effect on standards of better planning and co-operation in preparing a new curriculum as against freedom to spend money to meet specific needs, cannot be easy. We would, therefore, expect the *measurable* impact on examination results, for example, to be extremely difficult, if not impossible, to quantify. This difficulty is reflected in studies of delegated management in several countries.

An OECD (1994) synthesis of studies in nine countries on the effectiveness of schooling and education resource management, of which the study in this book was one, recognises the problem of assessing the effects of delegated resource management. It observes that researchers have: 'had difficulty demonstrating direct empirical links between school organisation and student outcomes, in part because the research to date has lacked the necessary depth and time scale to draw out such effects' (para. 21). The report does, however, go on to make a stronger case for greater approaches to 'autonomy' and greater 'participation', basing its comments on findings from the US study which claims 'enhanced effectiveness in both ethos or quality of learning, and in student outcomes'. Abstracting out differences between schemes of delegation, this leads to an a priori justification for extending forms of autonomy and the synthesis cites the studies undertaken in Australia, Spain and Germany (North-Rhine

Westphalia) as examples where the changes are likely to have a positive effect on student outcomes:

> where implemented under necessary conditions, greater autonomy in schools, as in the *Australia* study, '[leads] to greater effectiveness through greater flexibility in and therefore better use of resources; to professional development selected at school level; to more knowledge-able teachers and parents, so to better financial decisions; to whole-school planning and implementation with priorities set on the basis of data about student [outcomes and] needs'.

(para. 22)

Taken as a whole, however, the synthesis warns against drawing unprob-lematic conclusions. It argues that the prospects for autonomy leading to improvements in teaching and learning are contingent upon other changes, including appropriate training and continuing external support systems. Success is also seen as contingent upon external monitoring by central agencies and an emphasis upon a framework of partnership between a wide range of stakeholders. These comments are an appropriate reminder that delegation alone is no guarantee of improvement and recognises the need for organisational change to accompany delegation. Such 'theorising' about the organisational form of delegated management is informed by the wider literature on school management, school effectiveness and school improvement.

The internal management of delegation

Set against these uncertainties about the effects of delegated management, some theorists have, nonetheless, been confident in their assertions of its merits. Cheng (1993) begins by noting the limited number of articles which explain 'the concept and theory of school-based management and map its management characteristics of school functioning from an organizational perspective' (p.7). His own analysis is premised on the complex and unstable nature of the education environment and the multiplicity of educational goals. This leads to a view supporting decentralisation be-cause it allows problems to be solved where they occur, provides flex-ibility, responsibility and opportunity for individuals and organisations to use their initiative. It is a logic which has led some writers to claim that only markets – presented as the ultimate form of self-reliance and opportunity – can solve the problems of the school system (Chubb and Moe, 1990; Lieberman, 1993). While these latter critiques merit sustained discussion (see Bullock and Thomas, 1996) their concern is with the organisation of systems of schools, whereas our principal focus is with how schools might best be organised internally for managing resources for improvement. The two areas are, however, connected and, whilst we see benefit in *quasi*-market forms of organisations, our analysis leads us to conclude that there is a key role of system management which can add value to the performance of schools. It is an issue we consider in the concluding chapter.

Theorising that those closest to problems are best placed to resolve them is also reflected in the early and influential account by Caldwell and Spinks (1988). Its general model for school decentralisation proposes that effective self-management depends upon creating a context of collaborative management and a process of goal setting, planning, budgeting, implementing and evaluating. More recently, Caldwell (1994) continues to stress the potential of decentralisation and locates its significance within wider social restructuring. Many of the features of the Caldwell and Spinks model can be found in the guidance on development planning provided to all schools in England and Wales (DES, 1989; 1990), this approach also being represented in the school improvement study of development planning by Hargreaves and Hopkins (1991).

The underlying thesis of collaborative management presented in these models has resonance with the wider literature on school improvement. Fullan (1992) and Fullan and Hargreaves (1992) argue the case for collaboration and support greater school autonomy. Southworth (1994, p.52) suggests that 'staff in all schools should strive to make theirs a learning school' and identifies collaboration as a key characteristic. Dalin (1989, p.43) views 'collaborative efforts' as essential to successful change. An account of the 'Improving Education for All' (IQEA) Project observes how schools used development planning and

> as a result of the staff training day and the classroom observation, teachers began to talk more about teaching, collaborative work outside the project became more commonplace, and management structures were adapted to support this and future changes.
>
> (Hopkins and Ainscow, 1993, p.293)

An emphasis on collaboration and a focus upon the practice of teaching is also evident in studies of school effectiveness and are apparent in key British studies. The studies of 12 secondary schools reported by Rutter *et al.* (1979) and 50 junior schools reported by Mortimore *et al.* (1988) show more effective schools having these attributes. The study reported by Reynolds, Sullivan and Murgatroyd (1987) also shows the benefits of a focus upon the practice of teaching and, in their study, strategies for supporting the involvement of pupils. Since these studies of school effectiveness were undertaken before the introduction of LMS and GMS, theory building from their data cannot directly consider the effect of delegated resource management. More recent reports on school improvement, such as the IQEA Project and Quality Development in Birmingham (Burridge and Ribbins, 1994), focus on improvement strategies in schools but do not incorporate the role of resource management. It may be that they are right to do so! If delegated resource management has no great significance for school improvement, perhaps they are right to ignore it. But we ought to establish whether or not it is significant because the change has brought much additional work to schools.

On this theme, Davies and Hentshke (1994) observe: 'Developments in school autonomy have received enthusiastic promotion and support. But has anything significantly changed in the performance of schools?' (p.96). This leads to a 'critical taxonomy' intended to be a means of answering their question. But, while, the five areas of managerial decisions against which the 'reality' of autonomy might be assessed are legitimate enough, it is curious that the *effect* of these on the standard and quality of learning is not mentioned. This does not apply to a paper by Sharpe (1994) who proposes an extended framework against which devolution can be re-searched, classified and analysed. It recognises the place of student outcomes as a relevant variable and performance criterion and is an important antidote to analyses that overlook these effects which, as Knight (1993) recognises, have yet to be demonstrated.

Where does this bring us in terms of a research framework and methodology? There is clearly a requirement to work within an over-arching framework that incorporates *costs* and learning *outcomes*, because only then is it possible to take account of resource choices *and* their effect. Within that framework, the nature of the school as an organisation must be described. In varying degrees and in diverse ways, the literature on delegation, improvement and effectiveness recognises a relationship be-tween learning outcomes on the one side and, on the other, school (management) processes which emphasise participation and collabora-tion. In view of the attention given to development planning in England and Wales, by national policy and through professional development, we might expect it to be a means of participation.

We would also expect to see people other than teachers involved in the planning process. Taking account of the national legislative context, governors can be expected to have a role. It is they who are responsible for approving the Development Plan and the school budget. The role of parents, however, is more complex. The new legislative framework gives them a more active role in an accountability relationship with schools, as in the Annual Meeting with governors, and the new arrangements for school inspection invites them to give their views at a meeting and by survey. It is likely, therefore, that schools will be more alert to their views, an approach that would be consistent with evidence from some studies of school effectiveness. The Mortimore *et al.* (1988) study, for example, cites parental involvement as one of the key factors associated with effective schools. In view of this evidence and the legislative framework, therefore, it might be expected that cost-effective LMS and GMS will, at least, have policies which involve parents and will have means of regular communication with them.

As for pupils, the literature on effectiveness and improvement points to the importance of a positive ethos, shaping their attitudes and opinions. As reported in the Mortimore study, the more effective schools were those

> where teachers actively encouraged self-control on the part of pupils. . . . Positive effects resulted where teachers obviously enjoyed teaching their classes, valued the fun factor, and communicated their enthusiasm to the children. Their interest in the children as individuals, and not just as learners, also fostered progress. Those who devoted more time to non-school chat or small talk increased pupils' progress and development.
>
> (1988, p.255)

Under LMS and GMS, these attitudes might also be expected to be seen in the management of resources. Decisions on the use of resources should, in some cases, represent needs as perceived by pupils so that the cost-effective school will not only manifest positive teacher–pupil relationships in the classroom but will also deploy its new responsibilities over resources in ways that gives some recognition to the preferences of pupils.

How this empirical and theoretical evidence on approaches to the internal management of delegation is integrated into a specification of the cost-effective school is described in the next section. It includes an analytical discussion on the uncertainties associated with management and planning in schools which, we argue, adds to the case for more participatory approaches to school management.

THE COST-EFFECTIVE SCHOOL

We would expect the cost-effective school to use its responsibilities over resources to match educational needs and priorities. In this sense, delegated management enhances the educational role of managers in schools. Our overarching framework, therefore, provides a means for identifying the use of resources (costs) and their consequence for learning (effectiveness). In addition, however, and reflecting the wider literature, it needs to show the processes of decision making in order to ensure that we ask whether it is focused on learning, who is involved and the nature of that involvement.

A focus on learning

The standard and quality of learning must be the prime concern in any school in England and Wales. There is little benefit in having lengthy and high-sounding development plans for improving the school, for example, if they fail to be turned into everyday opportunities and achievements for pupils. For these reasons, Figure 3.1 has been designed to make a visually

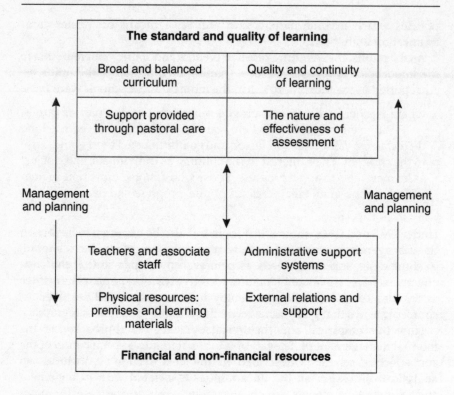

Figure 3.1 Linking resources to learning

explicit link between resources, resource management and educational standards and quality.

The figure gives primacy to learning and shows it as constituted by four components. The first recognises the importance of the National Curriculum and the statutory requirement for schools to provide a broad and balanced *curriculum*. Specifying the formal curriculum is no guarantee of quality and standards, as much also depends upon ensuring *continuity* between and within schools. As pupils move through their years in school, progression is assisted by their teachers being aware of completed programmes of work, previous achievements and difficulties. It avoids the twin problems of taking too much or too little for granted and can assist teachers in meeting the needs of individual pupils through effective and differentiated programmes. It is an area of activity long recognised as requiring attention at the stage of transfer between schools but it is no less important as pupils transfer between years within schools. The quality of information on the achievements and difficulties encountered by pupils will depend in part upon the nature and effectiveness of procedures for *assessment* and recording. These must fulfil statutory requirements but they must also do much more, providing diagnostic information which can assist teaching strategies. Much also depends on the support provided through *pastoral care* systems. These are not optional extras but are integral to the personal support provided for pupils both because pastoral care is right in itself and is instrumental in contributing to achieving the objectives of the formal curriculum.

If the standard and quality of learning can be described as being dependent upon the curriculum, continuity, assessment and pastoral care, they each depend upon the human and physical resources summarised in the second part of Figure 3.1. These are the means by which ideas become realities. *Teachers and associate staff* are the principal budgetary resource in schools. Their number, quality and commitment are central to achievement in any school. It is they who make a reality of the curriculum and assessment arrangements, the continuity of learning and the pastoral support. Improving schools must be aware of the attention they give to maintaining and developing the capacities, skills and commitment of their staff. If staff are fundamental we should not ignore the role of *administrative support*. Easy to criticise as an adjunct to the core activity of schools, it is administration that is critical, for example, in maintaining pupil records and enabling teachers to learn about the progress pupils have made in earlier years. The *physical resources* used by the school include learning resources and the premises occupied by the school. The number of science laboratories, for example, affects the nature of the science taught in schools and the scale, modernity and maintenance of equipment in the laboratories shape learning opportunities. The type and quality of buildings – some being hot in summer and cold in winter – affect the working conditions of all. Schools do not stand alone, all draw in *external support* in a variety of forms. This can include advice and support from LEAs or from services bought from a range of other public and private providers. External support also has a non-financial dimension. The support provided by parents must be recognised, whether it is in the form of unpaid help in schools or the more important out-of-school contribution to their children's aspirations and achievements. The non-financial dimension of all the human resources upon which schools depend merits emphasis. The contribution of teachers and associate staff, for example, cannot only be measured in terms of their budgetary cost; the goodwill they bring to their work will differ from one school to another and have an effect upon what a school can hope to achieve.

The final part of Figure 3.1 concerns the arrows showing *management and planning*, the means by which the link is made between resources and learning. Its location in the figure is intended to emphasise its place in schools: *distinctive* and *detached*. It is through systems of management and planning that schools define their aims and purposes and determine how best to achieve them. In this respect management and planning have a central and *distinctive* role. Paradoxically, they are also *detached* from the primary activity of teaching and learning. Management and planning is about setting objectives, preparing policies and planning how best to implement them; it is about allocating resources to tasks and monitoring whether objectives are being fulfilled. In this sense, management and planning is conceptually and practically distinct from the core activity of schools. Management and planning is not about actually doing the teaching and learning, which is not to say that teachers – and learners – cannot participate in them.

We present the role of management in this paradoxical form in order to stress two issues. The first is the importance of management. We have already indicated that management is distinctive and central in providing the arrangements by which schools make the link between resources on the one side and learning on the other. Ensuring that schools are teaching the right things and doing so in ways which make best use of available resources is of self-evident importance. The second is the danger of detachment. Since management is less about the doing of teaching and learning and more about agreeing purposes and ensuring that they are being achieved, there must be some concern that detachment does not become isolation from the principal means by which learning is achieved. Concern about detachment is all the greater for management in a school – as against many other organisations – because its people-changing purposes mean that outcomes are often difficult to measure. In effect, *uncertainty* is endemic to schools but the detachment of management adds to that uncertainty. In developing the implications of these issues for the cost-effective school but also because of its pervasiveness, we begin with development planning.

Development planning in the cost-effective school

The survey of 800 schools undertaken as part of the 'Impact' Project showed 95 per cent of schools with Development Plans and head teachers reported favourably on them. The process of preparing a plan has a set of distinctive stages and the already extensive literature providing guidance and commentary on the planning process as a whole does not need addition. Our contribution is to consider how development planning for the cost-effective school might be expected to differ from planning for the effective school.

Four stages characterise the conventional cycle of development planning. These are:

- the need for *audit* in order to review the school's current strengths and weaknesses in relation to its aims;
- identifying *priorities* which will allow the school to close the gap between its current position and its intended objectives;

- deciding upon the best means for *implementing* proposed changes; and
- ensuring that progress is being reliably *evaluated*.

While these stages are conceptually distinct, we do not assume or expect that they are so easily distinguished in practice. The process of audit in some schools, for example, may become interwoven with discussion and agreement on priorities for the forthcoming year. There is little doubt, also, that the process of implementation cannot easily or usefully be separated from evaluation, the latter often having only the appearance of occurring at the end of a planning cycle. More likely, evaluation – how are we doing? – proceeds in parallel with implementation and often leads to worthwhile changes from those originally proposed. Evaluation also provides much of the audit data for the subsequent cycle, eroding in practice the conceptual distinction. How these stages of development planning occur will, therefore, differ among schools and we should not expect a conceptual distinction to be mirrored by reality. This does not mean that development planning is not occurring and, if schools are properly engaged in the activity, we would expect a researcher to be able to analyse events in the schools and identify the key stages of planning. This also means that we should be able to distinguish the characteristics of development planning in effective as against cost-effective schools.

The sequence and stages of development planning are likely to be similar in effective schools and cost-effective schools. We would, however, expect different questions to be asked at the audit stage in the cost-effective school. Figure 3.1 in this chapter provides a guide for auditing different aspects of work in a school, inviting a review of those facets of work that contribute to the standard and quality of learning. In terms of monitoring effectiveness, it refers to the collection and use of information on the practice of teaching and learning. Such a review contributes to the identification of implications for resources, as occurs when new developments in the curriculum require some preparatory development work by teachers. In this respect, practice in the cost-effective school would be little different from practice in the effective school. What would be expected to distinguish the cost-effective school would be its readiness to go further in its audit of the match between curriculum requirements and resources. As with an effective school, there will be a concern to fill any evident gap in staff expertise in the curriculum but it will, periodically, also undertake a more fundamental review.

A major staff audit, for example, would assess which tasks currently undertaken by members of the teaching staff might equally well be done by others who are less costly to employ. How much work in science, for example, could be undertaken by a science technician, releasing teacher time for activities more appropriate to the science teacher's expertise? There may be circumstances where teachers with responsibility for the science curriculum assess that the next science vacancy could be filled by a combination of a part-time teacher and a technician, the combined costs of which being no greater than a full-time teacher. Because technicians are less costly to employ than teachers, the change not only employs people with the right skills but also increases the hours of staff time available to support the curriculum.

In the cost-effective school, this principle of what might be called a *radical audit* would also apply to other resources. It would involve creativity and diversity in the use of premises, the development of administrative systems and support, as well as a more extensive use of external resources than is normally the case. In effect, the cost-effective school is more likely to consider and introduce innovative ways of working that involve changes in the conventions and routines of schools. Such changes may be as likely to arise in decisions on approaches to teaching and the management of learning as in the use and deployment of resources.

Radical audit has implications for the setting of priorities. If schools are considering innovative ways of working, the case for assessing their costs and benefits is more obvious, although no more necessary than ensuring that current practice is cost-effective. This has implications for good information on costs, recognition of forgone alternatives as well as anticipated benefits. Figure 3.2 shows a proforma prepared for an earlier study for reporting on costs and recording anticipated benefits. (Mortimer and Mortimer with Thomas 1994) It is a more formal report than we might expect schools to develop but it illustrates the need for reviewing costs and benefits during discussion of priorities.

(Figures include on-costs)		
Post	Non-teaching assistants (10 part-time posts)	Source of funds: school budget share
Salary	£25,000 p.a.	Benefits: 110 hours per week of non-teaching classroom support. Support for pupils across ability range. Assist teachers with reading, resources and administration
Premises Equipment Supervision	None specified None specified £2,600	
Total recurrent costs	£27,600 p.a.	

Figure 3.2 Reviewing costs and benefits

Effective and cost-effective schools would ensure that priorities are set, means of implementation agreed and progress evaluated. Unlike differences at the audit stage of development planning, and the appraisal of costs and benefits to which we have referred, we would not expect these other stages to differ, although greater innovation is likely to require a longer period of planning and implementation. However, we do not assume that if all these processes are in place there will always be an effect in the classroom. The difficulties of securing a planning process which has these features and has an effect on the classroom are recognised in some recent work on development planning (Mortimore, MacGilchrist and Savage, 1995). The process does, however, have the potential for securing collaborative working and closing the gap between management and classroom practice. In this way, it provides a means for reducing the uncertainty and detachment of school management. That it is not sufficient to do this brings us to other characteristics of management in the cost-effective school.

Uncertainty and the management of resources for learning

Given the absence of a specific and predictive theory of learning, decisions about learning strategies and the choice of resources in support of those strategies will be based upon judgement. That this should be so not only affirms our common-sense awareness about the role of judgement in an activity like teaching but also has implications for management decisions in schools. This applies to decisions on resource allocation, teaching strategies and assessments of their effect on learning.

Levels of delegation

In making decisions on the school budget, judgements are required on the balance of spending between different resources. There are no guidelines on the proportion of a budget which should be spent, for example on teachers as against support staff. We cannot predict the circumstances when it is more sensible to spend rather more or rather less on books. Such circumstances go some way to justifying the delegation of decisions on resources, as it is assumed that those at school level are better informed about local needs. In this respect, delegation of management decisions to lower levels is an implicit recognition that management can be too detached and not have enough information for sound decisions. We should recognise, however, that there is no guarantee that being close to local circumstances always leads to better decisions. This may occur because some are poor judges of needs and others poor at judging the best way of meeting them. For these reasons, it is sensible that decisions on resource choices are not restricted to too few people.

We must also recognise that the most suitable mix of resources not only will differ as between schools – the case for delegation to the school site – but will also differ between year groups, subjects and other school activities. That is, the mix of resources required for cost-effective learning in mathematics, for example, may differ between Year 8 and 11 and each may differ from the needs of science. It would seem sensible, therefore, for the expertise of relevant teaching staff to inform decisions on the allocation of resources. To do so is to do no more than recognise that the senior managers in schools can be detached and lack adequate knowledge of practice. If these conditions contribute to the case for delegation and for that to be extended within the school, we should be alert to its limits. Not only must delegation be distinguished from autonomy but we must also be cautious about the expertise of professionals.

Delegation not autonomy

Autonomy involves a recognition that in certain areas of action, individuals or groups have a right to self-determination. It is they who decide upon these courses of action and are not answerable to others for their choice. In the context of funding locally managed schools, for example, LEAs are allowed autonomy in deciding the relative funding level of children of different ages. Whether their decisions are acceptable or not, constitutionally, is a matter for them and their local electorate. In other words, even here, autonomy is constrained as it is the electorate who have the right of self-determination.

The delegation of resource management to schools must be distinguished from this kind of autonomy for LEAs. Their right to make their own spending decisions is contingent upon it being used responsibly. First, decisions on resources must be taken in the context of a primary statutory duty to implement the National Curriculum; spending decisions must give primacy to meeting the requirements of the National Curriculum. Second, the continued right to delegation is contingent upon how it is exercised; if schools plan to overspend their budget, for example, an LEA has a duty to suspend the powers of delegation. Third, the exercise of their powers is subject to a regular financial audit and a four-yearly inspection. The latter leads to a published report which includes a judgement on how well resources are being used and whether the school is providing value for money. In extreme cases of poor management, the head and governing body can be replaced. If these brief examples illustrate the difference of principle between autonomy and delegation, we must recognise that, nonetheless, on a day-to-day basis school managers have considerable discretion and freedom of action. This brings us to the limits of professional expertise.

Using Figure 3.1 as a guide, the evidence upon which resource needs must be based is an assessment of the standard and quality of learning. The source of this evidence is normally the teachers themselves. It can arise, however, that teachers in a subject department or in the school as a whole may have become complacent about standards and quality and, that being so, mistakenly assess needs. Outside observers, for example, might take the view that improvements in the teaching in a subject department could occur with suitable professional development provision, a need which is not recognised by those teachers. In effect, for teachers and for schools as a whole, freedom of action – what we typically call professional autonomy – must depend upon how well they exercise that freedom. Inspection of schools is one formal and infrequent way of ensuring that this freedom is being used to good effect. Routinely also, head teachers are responsible for the conduct and decisions of other staff in the school and all are overseen by a governing body. As the senior management of the school, both groups – head teachers and governing bodies – have a central role in ensuring quality and standards but both face the problem of being detached from the core activities which secure learning.

We are presented with a dilemma for resource management in schools. Senior management is detached from the core practice of schools and the principal sources of its information may not always be the best judges of need. How that dilemma might be overcome depends upon creating a dialogue of accountability.

Enabling a dialogue

Schools need structures and processes whereby decisions about the allocation of resources are made in ways that are well informed about the standard and quality of the core activities which support learning: decisions based upon poor information can lead to a mismatch of resources to needs. However, the information required is predominantly qualitative and its principal sources – teachers and head teachers – may sometimes not be the best judges of need. We suggest that resolving this dilemma has three main components, all of which are related to the nature and quality of information. These are: the structure of decision making; the dialogue between interested groups; and the sources of information.

Since the purpose of delegating resource management is to improve the match between resources and educational needs, the structures for decision making must provide for a link between those aspects of school life. The governing body is accountable for resources and learning and any committee structure that is created should ensure that decisions about resources are properly informed by an assessment of educational need. As much is true for any whole school committees of which senior staff and others are members and it is also the case for decisions within faculties or subject departments. In undertaking our study, therefore, one of the areas we monitored was the nature of the decision-making structure on resources and, in the three case study schools, we attended meetings of governors, senior staff, faculties and departments.

At those meetings as well as in other contexts, the nature of the dialogue over resources and educational needs is a crucial test of accountability. If meetings of governors with head teachers, alone or with other teachers, consist of the teachers talking and governors quietly agreeing with their advice, they can scarcely be described as dialogues. Even so, *listening* can be a means of some accountability. The very fact that head teachers and teachers must give an account of their plans to governors and get their support requires them to review their circumstances and come with a reasoned case. Their decisions may be all the better for that; all the more if governors have the ability and the confidence to discuss the proposals being brought to them, as the quality of the replies provide a further test of the quality of the proposals. Within schools, the quality of the internal dialogue – senior staff alone or with heads of department or of departmental staff – is a test of internal professional accountability. Are meetings characterised by discussion or do they involve more senior staff telling less senior staff; are they predominantly about procedural and administrative activities or do they discuss aspects of teaching and learning? When they discuss resource priorities, to what extent is evidence on needs and priorities in teaching and learning drawn upon? The extent to which this occurs is an indicator that these areas are being linked and that management is resolving the problem of its detachment. These questions provide some criteria by which these meetings can be monitored and provide a basis for our qualitative assessment. A further criterion in that assessment would be the sources of information used in these meetings.

The significance of information for decisions in this area cannot be understated. If management is to meet the challenge of its structural detachment from practice, it requires good quality information. Much of that information will be reported by the professionals most closely involved in the activity. The views of head teachers and teachers on needs will often be based upon sound assessments and the quality of their judgements will be tested in the meetings we have been describing. Within these professional groups in recent years, the quality of this information has been enhanced by the growth of team approaches to curriculum planning. The introduction of appraisal is also making teachers more accustomed to observing their colleagues' practice. Nevertheless, that it is teachers who provide the main source of information about educational needs remains an issue, and only partly because they may not always be reliable sources of evidence. The views of pupils – the learners – is a neglected source of evidence. They are experienced observers of teachers in schools but their views are seldom sought in any systematic way. For these reasons, we conclude that evidence collected directly from pupils provides an important source of information on aspects of teaching and learning, and school life more generally. We do not propose this as a means of *policing* the teaching in schools but to provide a commentary on the school and its provision which is distinctive from that of the professionals. How pupil surveys, as well as those for teachers and parents, can be developed and used is demonstrated by work undertaken for the Scottish Office (1992a; 1992b). Their use has an added benefit because it provides a source of information which is independent of the head teacher and the teachers. In this respect, it may inform them of views from a different perspective, as well as providing governors with a further source of information that is independent of the head teacher and teachers. Such a source of information enriches the evidence base on the core activity of schools and is a means by which the detachment of management can be further reduced.

Our use of parent and pupil surveys in this study, therefore, is more than a research technique but is itself a statement about how schools can add to their information base and ensure that in managing their resources, they are matching resources to needs. This brings us to the resource choices themselves and the extent to which schools are aware of options in spending decisions and their costs.

Options and their costs

One source of data on delegated management is the resource choices actually made by schools. If schools do not use these responsibilities to make decisions which differ from those made by the LEA, the case for delegation must be weakened. Even where they do make different decisions, however, it is appropriate to examine the nature of the options considered. This means learning more about the way governors, head teachers and others perceive the choices available to them. For example, is delegation making schools more innovative in the way they spend money or do they spend more (or less) on the same type of resources as in the past? There are a number of texts which have examined this issue and argued for the greater use of support staff who would be employed to do some work that may traditionally have been done by teachers (Barber and Brighouse, 1992; HMI, 1992; Mortimore and Mortimore with Thomas, 1994). Are schools actually making these types of appointments and how are they affecting practice in schools? Appointing a classroom assistant, for example, is no guarantee of improvements in the classroom if teachers are not skilled at making use of the assistance.

Related to the exercise of choice is information on its costs. Evidence from a number of sources suggest that schools rarely consider the range of costs involved in some of their decisions. In his contribution to a study on the innovative uses of non-teaching staff in schools, Hywel Thomas developed and applied a methodology for identifying a range of costs associated with these new posts. It also provided information on the source of funding – by no means always the school budget – and the benefits claimed for the changes (Mortimore and Mortimore with Thomas, 1994). What was apparent from the data collection was the limited range of costs identified by each school. Each was able to give information on the salary costs of post(s) but those associated with provision of accommodation, equipment and management had to be prepared specially for the study.

This limited conception of costs is reinforced by the design and use of much financial management information for schools. This is normally presented showing costs under traditional budget headings – teachers, clerical staff, energy, maintenance and so on – rather than identifying costs to specific centres. As a result, schools are now encouraged to develop their financial information in ways that allow them to compare, for example, the overall costs of different subjects. Tradition is a powerful factor here and our contacts with the principal supplier of financial information systems to schools (School Management Information Systems or SIMS) show schools reluctant to develop cost-centred information systems even though the option is available.

Taken together, consideration of options and their costs are integral to creative and cost-effective use of delegated powers. Options and their costs add to the information for the judgements upon which decisions ultimately rest in the cost-effective management of resources.

The cost-effective schools summarised

In the preceding sections, our concern has been two-fold. First, we set out a framework which emphasises the link between resources and learning. Second, we observed that decisions on how best to use resources for learning are made by a management system which is detached from the core activity of schools, where information is not always reliable and is seldom sufficiently independent in its origin. This led us to consider, third, the implications of these conditions for managing for cost-effectiveness.

In summarising these implications, our intention is to complement the existing state of knowledge about effective schools. Our summary should be read in conjunction with the principal conclusions of that literature and not as an alternative. The focus on purpose, participation and practice in the 12 factors of *School Matters*, for example, is wholly consistent with our own commentary and our concern for effective schools to be cost-effective. In adding to the attributes which lead to effectiveness, however, the cost-effective school will:

• Periodically undertake a *radical audit* of resources, particularly in the use of staff. Use of premises would be characterised by creativity and diversity. Decisions on resources will differ from the past and the audit of professional development needs must take this into account.

- Improve information on *costs*. Financial information is more likely to be cost-centred. Choices will be assessed in terms of an awareness of forgone opportunities and their benefits.
- Use the expertise of relevant staff on resource priorities through some *internal delegation* of decision making on resources.
- Limit the dangers of complacency about standards and quality by ensuring that the structure of decision making provides for a *dialogue of accountability* of high quality.
- Reduce the *detachment of management* by using team meetings, appraisal and surveys to collect information on the quality of teaching and learning from teachers, parents and pupils.
- Develop sources of information which are *independent* of head teachers and teachers.

THE STRUCTURE AND METHODOLOGY OF THE STUDY

In the chapters which follow, we report the evidence collected from 18 secondary schools identified as likely exemplars of good practice in their management of resources in terms of school improvement. Clearly, they are potentially cost-effective schools. Our aim is to report on their practice and, *inter alia*, comment upon their practice. Since our design of the study was informed by our thinking on the cost-effective school, it is appropriate that we explain our stages of data collection and analysis and explain its relationship with our model of the cost-effective school. In doing so, readers should be advised that, while its essential features are unchanged, our conception of the cost-effective school has been refined as our own work has progressed. The enquiry was divided into three phases.

In Phase 1, we developed Figure 3.1 for use as a basis for the collection of data. The specification of this framework was a critical first phase of the project as it was the basis for shaping the focus of our data collection, a guide in the preparation of our interview schedules and for determining the criteria used for examining and reporting on the schools and their management of resources. The framework also assisted the process of identifying exemplar schools, for which the field knowledge of HMI was a critical input. The 18 secondary schools selected were not a sample in any statistical sense but are intended to illustrate good practice. In this respect they reflect a tradition of enquiry of which, in this context, *Ten Good Schools* (HMI, 1977) is a good illustration. As these schools were intended to illustrate good practice, our concern was to identify a set of schools which presented circumstances where the new responsibilities were being used to enhance educational effectiveness. The final part of our work in this phase was the preparation of schedules of questions for the first round of school visits.

In our question schedules, we emphasised the kinds of resource choices made in the schools and how changes directly affected the process of teaching and learning. How pupils experience the consequence of resource choices in LMS and GMS must be one of the tests of delegation. In seeking views, our focus was on assessments of quality as against the measurement of standards. This is partly because the project's resources would not have allowed a large scale quantitative study but, more important, we would not expect to separate *measured* changes in pupil outcomes from the effects of other contemporary changes. In defining our approach to the collection of qualitative data on the relationship between delegation and quality, it was evident that there was comparatively little guidance in the literature. The impact of delegation on resource choices and on the quality of student experiences in schools remains a neglected area of enquiry.

In Phase 2, we planned and undertook field visits to the 18 selected schools. These were normally one-day visits but two days were required in some cases. During these visits we conducted over 100 interviews and collected relevant documents, such as Development Plans, budgets and school prospectuses. We sought interviews with the same categories of people in each school: head teacher, deputy head teacher, head of the mathematics department and the head of the history department. Given the role of governing bodies in schools in England and Wales, we secured interviews with the Chair of the governing body and an elected parent governor. About six interviews were undertaken in a single-day visit to each school, using interview schedules which were sent in advance. The method can be described as the use of a *supported self-completed interview schedule*. Interviewees had the opportunity to consider their views before-hand and, at the meeting with the interviewer, they had the opportunity to clarify ambiguities and uncertainties. The visit also allowed us to collect necessary information on curriculum, resources and management systems. Occasionally, individuals were followed up by means of telephone inter-views. The field visit data were then subject largely to qualitative analysis, identifying examples of how the schools used their new responsibilities, the processes of decision making and the effect of changes on the experiences of pupils. It should be apparent from this that the framework in Figure 3.1 provided a structure which informed that analysis. An aspect of the analysis also examined differences between LMS and GMS arising from their different circumstances. It was following the analyses of these data that we identified three improving schools for more detailed study.

Phase 3 began with preparatory work for the field visits to the three case study schools. A minimum of ten days was earmarked for each school with visits spread over a number of weeks. More teachers were interviewed together with members of the non-teaching staff. The visits were arranged so that meetings could be observed, including meetings of governors. Visits were spread to allow attendance at meetings at different stages of activity in the year. Allowing time between interviews also enabled us to reflect upon earlier interviews. In these schools, we conducted over 70 interviews and attended 26 meetings.

Arrangements were also made for collecting the views of parents and students. Schedules of statements were prepared for students in Year 9 and their parents. Each schedule was unique to the school in that statements were designed to represent special initiatives in each school. They did, however, include statements which were common to all schools. Questionnaires were returned from 313 parents, a 50 per cent response, and 521 pupils, an 84 per cent response. As with the data set of 18 school visits, the data from the three improving schools were largely subject to qualitative analysis with quantitative methods used as appropriate. Interviews were based upon schedules of questions and, like the first set of visits, these were pre-circulated. This was followed by the analysis and writing up of the case studies of the three schools. The project concluded with the preparation of a final report integrating material on the context of reform, existing literature and the two types of school-based material (Thomas and Martin, 1994).

In ways that reflect our view about the uncertainties associated with cost-effectiveness in schools, we view our own results, at best, as *illuminating* the issue of the relationship between education resource management and the standard and quality of learning. We can point to changes in the classroom experiences of students but we cannot show any measured increments of learning. We can show quantitative data on student and parent opinions but we must be cautious in our assessment of their significance as expressions of final outcomes. They do, nonetheless, offer some insight into the perspectives and experiences of these groups. We might summarise our approach as one which places a reliance upon accounts of school processes but which are sensitive to the limitations of material.

CONCLUSION

Delegating more responsibility over resources to the school site is an international phenomenon and there is a growing literature on how that might be done and its effects on schools. In this chapter, our intention has been to make a distinctive contribution to that literature, first, by recognising the pre-eminence of pupil learning in assessing the effects of delegation and, second, by exploring the organisational implications of the uncertainties attendant on the management of resources in schools. It has also located the analysis in the specific developments in England and Wales and we urge caution for drawing comparisons with other national initiatives. Even where there appear to be strategic similarities between national schemes of delegation, the devil is in the detail and such detail makes schemes unique. By adding to that a recognition of cultural differences among nations, caution must inform our tendencies and desires to generalise.

The analysis provides a framework for assessing practice and it is to the cases selected as examples of good practice that we now turn. From 15 schools – 11 LM and four GM – there are instances of practice showing, in specific areas of school activity, the relationship between resource management and educational effectiveness. Chapter 4 is not an account of circumstances in a whole school but illustrates ways in which schools have used their new responsibilities, how decisions were made and what effect they had on pupils. The accounts from Chapters 5, 6 and 7 on each of the three improving schools, however, are intended to reflect developments across the school as a whole. These case studies are also intended to give insight into the ways in which the specific context of a school and the different responsibilities of LM as against GM schools affect their work and performance.

Part II

Resourcing improvement in practice

Chapter 4

Managing resources for improvement in 15 schools

The 15 schools discussed in this chapter demonstrate the extent to which the powers granted to schools by LMS and GMS are being used to develop and improve the provision and opportunities for their students. During interviews with over 90 people we were given a wide variety of examples of how the new responsibilities for resource management were being used. Some of these many examples have been organised into four sections, each representing different types of resources: staffing, administration and infrastructure, environment and learning materials. These are followed by a section which examines the use of external sources of funding which are distinct from the school's basic formula-based budget. It is our assessment that the diversity of these revenue sources constitute, in some degree, innovative practices. We suggest that the greater autonomy and accountability for finance and financial management at the level of the school is contributing to a more entrepreneurial approach, where schools are seeking new sources of funding. In all these five sections we not only cite examples of change but endeavour to report how the schools assessed their effect upon the learning experiences of the students.

These examples of how delegated management is being used is prefaced, however, by an examination of the decision-making processes which link resources to learning in these schools. Our purpose in this section is to *illuminate* good practice rather than to make over-ambitious claims about explaining complex relationships. This emphasis is all the more important given that here we draw upon information collected by spending a day in each school, the analysis of relevant documents and interviews with about six people in each school. In the concluding section, we reflect on this evidence in terms of our concept of the cost-effective school. A brief biography of all these schools, together with the three case study schools, is provided in the Appendix.

PROCESSES OF SCHOOL DECISION MAKING

Many studies have reported on the important role of school leadership and management in contributing to effective schools. It is appropriate, therefore, to begin this review of good practice in the 15 schools by examining the processes of decision making in education resource management. To what extent do these schools exhibit purposeful leadership, linked to a clear set of aims and priorities for their development? What is the place of development planning in this part of school management, given its contemporary prominence? Given the nature of the changes, what is the role of governors and governing bodies? Who is involved in making decisions and what, in particular, is the role of the head teacher? These are all questions which are considered, albeit briefly, in the first part of our account. It is followed by one part which examines changes in the processes of decision making as a consequence of greater delegation and a final part which considers whether these processes differ between those schools which are locally managed and those which are grant maintained.

The character of decision making

Purposeful leadership

The evidence from our one-day visits certainly indicates a set of schools which exhibit a sense of purposeful leadership in their management of resources. Almost without exception, those questioned had little difficulty identifying decisions on resources which were consistent with a wider and coherent framework of aims and priorities for the school. These aims are mentioned in a variety of ways, sometimes in the same school. At School 12, for example, the head teacher referred to the 'whole school thrust towards individualised learning – agreed with staff, governors and translated into organisation by the Management Team'. He also observed that the policy on joint use of school and community resources was made clear by him at his interview: 'stated at interview – priority if appointed – pursued ever since'. An interview with one of the deputies illustrated the organisational implications of the policy on individualised learning: 'School policy to decide to keep groups small to optimise learning possibilities – involvement in flexible learning project made it an important element'. An interview with a second deputy provided several examples of ways in which youth, community, further and higher education services were integrated with the school's provision so that overall provision benefited through more effective use of facilities. Delegation was seen as enabling such integration to take place.

In School 5, development planning was the language through which purpose was expressed, the head teacher's account emphasising his role in setting the framework: 'SDP – I wrote the aims, worked on goals and objectives with Heads of Faculty'. In School 1, development planning was also the language used for giving expression to purpose. As the head teacher commented at one stage, 'like all our developments it is a standard process', and went on to give an account which located decision making through an explicit process of development planning.

That we have given prominence to the views of the head teachers in the setting of aims and purposes is no more than a reflection of their role in these schools. It should not be assumed, however, that this typifies wider processes of decision making. The interviews report a wide range of people involved in decisions and a variety of processes by which they are involved. Among these, development planning was prominent.

Decisions through development planning

Development planning was often a process which complemented the structure of committees, such as the Senior Management Team (SMT), Academic Boards and heads of department meetings. Comments from School 6 illustrate the place of development plans (school and departmental) as a framework for linking resources to educational needs. One head of department commented:

> The SDP has driven the decisions, which has drawn on the departmental development plan. There is, for example, a rolling programme of refurbishment and a rolling programme of funding as national curriculum subjects come on stream. The department requested new texts in their development plan. The department was given the money for furniture and we made our own decisions on how to spend this for the Humanities suite.

At the same school, the comments of another head of department show the relationship between departmental plans and the SMT: 'I put in a departmental development plan to expand the facility. This was picked up by the SMT and agreed.' These are comments echoed by a deputy:

> The SDP sets out the aims and objectives for the school and is produced by the SMT, which is informed by department development plans. 'SDP is a working document'. I can put my hand on my heart and say this.

The process of participation through planning can be quite elaborate. In School 8, questionnaires are distributed to staff and a half day set aside each year to re-examine/audit the Development Plan. Consultative processes through this and other means were mentioned by all those interviewed, one head of department commenting: 'We are extremely well informed. There is no feeling that senior management are taking all the decisions.' Another listed a set of working parties and committees which identify needs which have resource implications and noted that 'it is up to the SMT to decide on priorities'. Generally, specially constituted working parties are not common, brief reference being made in School 8 and School 4.

School 4 is distinctive for the role of the Financial and Management Committee (FMC). While this is a committee of the governing body its membership includes staff representatives elected by the whole staff. It is unusual, as it is mentioned by almost all those interviewed, teachers and governors. The head teacher referred to it as 'the main decision-making body. The full governing body only ratifies decisions.' It clearly has a significant resource management role, reflected by the comments of one deputy: 'Environment might be a priority – a decision perhaps taken at SMT. If it has significant financial implications then this must go to governors' FMC.' FMC receives advice from the head teacher, deputies and staff through a range of other structures and processes which include the preparation of a Development Plan. This was not typical of the accounts we received of the role of governors.

The role of governors

The joint membership of FMC in School 4 is uncommon as, indeed, that it is mentioned as a key committee by teachers and governors alike. School 7 provides a further interesting example of joint membership of committees. The Chair of governors described the decision to discontinue a committee structure and link governors to working groups based upon the aims identified for the Development Plan. Governors are also attached to departments to facilitate greater involvement.

More typical are circumstances where teachers refer to some committees and governors to others. The role of the governing body and of committees of the governing body is mentioned in all the schools but mainly by the governors whom we interviewed and by senior staff. The replies from the interviews at School 3, for example, show senior staff and governors referring to the role of governors but no mention of governors from the two heads of department. Even when they are mentioned by a head of department, information about them and their role is not well understood. At School 10, a head of department cited the allocation by the governing body of £25,000 specifically for books: 'Governors seem to have a pot of money to target a particular area, which they appear to have accumulated'.

By contrast, senior staff refer a good deal to governors being involved in making decisions, although we should recognise the extent of advice and guidance which they receive from their senior professionals. This does not mean that governors simply do as they are told. In many cases, the accounts suggest positive working partnerships where governors make a distinctive contribution. This can include individual governors providing resources through their own employment (School 8). It includes governors acting as 'critical friends', questioning the head teacher about proposals. Two examples give an insight into these relationships, in two schools where the governors clearly had the highest regard for their head teacher. In one, School 12, we were given an account of the review by the governing body of the annual examination results. While these results were good, it was clear that the governors interpreted their role as one of careful monitoring of performance. In School 13, where the enthusiasm for the head teacher could scarcely be greater, the governors closely questioned him on proposals to maintain the teaching complement at a level which they thought was rather tight. They had also been insistent over the appointment of a financial manager, an issue where the head teacher had shown a reluctance and required some persuasion.

The pivotal role of the Head

In all 15 schools what emerges from the interviews is the pivotal role of the head teacher in giving shape and direction to developments in his or her school. It is evident in accounts given by head teachers about the setting of school aims, goals and objectives. As significant, however, are the references to the head teacher by others whom we interviewed. In all schools, except one, the head teacher alone is mentioned as the decision-maker in one context or another. This is sometimes recognised by the head teacher, as in the comment from School 9: 'When I arrived, the school was at the point of closure. As a Head I had to react very quickly as there was no time to wait for decisions to be made.' Elsewhere, there are many examples of teachers taking proposals to the Head who gives approval. Equally, there are examples where the Head is the person who suggests new ideas and generates innovation.

Only in School 1 does the head teacher not appear as a figure mentioned as a key figure, which is not to say that he is not a key participant. Rather, the accounts mention the SMT (Senior Management Team), development planning for the school and its departments as well as other structures and processes for consultation. One head of department commented:

We do have Heads of Department meetings and Heads of Year meetings – chaired by the Head. Pastoral and Academic Heads are split between the two deputies and meet about once per month for Curriculum Development Meetings. We also have departmental meetings. The system of meetings enables consultation and briefing of staff concerning management decisions. A consultation process is in place which includes decisions on the use of resources. The Head has an open-door policy and an open style of management.

Such comments indicate that while the head teacher is pivotal it does not mean the head teacher decides alone. The role of the SMT is also prominent in most schools and is the key group in shaping decisions in many. Its membership is typically the head teacher and deputies and, in several schools, the senior teachers. In School 12, the SMT's prominence in policy decisions on curriculum and resource priorities was attested by the accounts of all the teachers interviewed. In School 10, the SMT (five people) meets to discuss proposals for the budget before they are put to the governing body, and its weekly meetings are clearly important events in the calendar. The replies of one deputy identified the SMT as the decision-making body for all the examples of resource choices which he mentioned.

In this section, we have focused upon how decisions over resources were made in the 15 schools. It remains for us to give an account of whether decisions differ between resource areas and how greater delegation has affected decision making.

Decisions and delegation

How decisions on resources are made does depend upon the type, purpose and significance of the resource. In effect, schools make spending decisions on the staff appointments in different ways to decisions on redecorating classrooms. Our data also do suggest some clear differences of approach within and between schools.

On issues such as increasing staff numbers, replacements and dismissals, proposals come from the full-time professionals and, typically, from the head teacher and/or SMT. The major decisions on the full complement of staff derive from an analysis of curriculum needs and available budgets and this information is mainly in the hands of the senior management of the school. In some schools, it is apparent that delegation has given these senior managers a much greater sense of control. Their curriculum analysis can now be the basis for their staffing policy and not the outcome of a staffing establishment fixed by the LEA. The educational and budgetary significance of these decisions leads to the involvement of heads of department and the governing body at various stages. The latter is clearly involved, both in the process of approving decisions in principle and subsequent actions, such as making a staff appointment.

When staffing decisions are more marginal, in the sense of a little more or less of a particular category of staff, the role of the Head remains pivotal but procedures are less formal. Thus, a head of department may suggest a development and the head teacher may respond positively, thereby legitimating its progress into the more formal processes of the school. The audit process of development planning can also lead to important development in the marginal allocation of staff. In some schools, this was the means by which additional clerical staff were appointed in order to provide support for the teaching staff.

In the main, however, decisions on administrative support are the domain of senior management. It is senior management which recognises needs in this area and proposes to governors that resources be earmarked. Our analysis of the interview schedules and our own notes show this to be an area where the head teacher and/or the SMT make proposals to the governing body with other staff not being at all clear how these decisions are made. In School 3, for example, the introduction of additional resources for management information was the result of a management review by the SMT working with the bursar. In School 7, the head teacher identified the increase in administrative staff as 'the most significant change', adding: 'My initiative to change. It was in the SDP and the governors recognise this. Other staff also recognise but some don't understand.'

Making proposals and setting priorities for the development of the school environment show the academic staff taking a leading role. Ideas and suggestions may come through informal suggestions or, more formally, through the audit part of development planning or as part of a long-term rolling programme of refurbishment. Brought together and costed they may be recommended to a committee of the governing body. As later sections of this chapter testify, there are many examples of improvements to premises which are relatively minor in cost but are important developments for the school.

The scale of a development can influence the way a decision is made but we should also recognise the complexity of some innovations. At School 6, plans to develop an arts suite were potentially expensive with suggested costs of £35,000. The head teacher took the lead and was able to secure a quotation for £15,000. The interview shows that there was more at stake, however, since the head teacher wanted to move towards a more integrated approach to the teaching of art, ceramics and textiles. The development of the accommodation was, therefore, part of a wider strategy for challenging existing teaching practices and the views of some members of staff on the direction of new developments.

Management responsibility for the environment was often the major role of a senior member of the academic staff. In School 10 this role was taken by a vice-principal. School 8 employs a property bursar for 2.5 days per week who is given an annual budget for maintenance but, before taking early retirement, he was a deputy head at the school. The budget is spent as part of a rolling programme of refurbishment and the school uses the money to mix/match an LEA capital programme which is in progress. The property bursar recommends priorities to the SMT.

The role of the academic staff dominates decisions on the purchase of learning materials. It is an area where the nature of decision making in these schools may be changing with a shift to allocating funds by a formula. It is a theme which is considered more fully in the chapter's section on learning materials.

Attracting resources from outside the school is an area where there is no dominant pattern of involvement in decisions. This could have much to do with the diversity of initiatives. Where there was much activity directed towards raising funds, notably matched-funding projects at School 6, the head teacher is a key figure. At School 12, the deputy head (community) was an important figure in developing a wider programme of further education, partly through the provision of courses franchised by the local college of further and higher education. This is an area where individual members of the governing body contribute through their own employment. School 5 benefited from the gift of a van from the manufacturing company where a governor was employed. In School 13, an Industry Day at the school arose from an original suggestion by a governor to the governing body's School and Industry Link Committee.

In the first two sections we have described who is involved in decision making, how decisions are made and whether involvement in decisions depends upon the type of educational resource. Our interview records suggest that important changes have occurred in the structure and process of decision making.

Changing structures and processes in decision making

On structure, the roles of governors and committees of the governing body are among the major changes. We have already described ways in which they are involved and our interviews include many references to committees – notably finance and premises – whose existence and role are a consequence of greater delegation. In School 7, their new role had led to a review. Governors now met once a term for their normal business meeting and once a term for a seminar which audited/reviewed work on the Development Plan. The responsibilities of governing bodies for resources also mean that they are not only informed of developments but required to give their approval. This has brought individual members of the governing body and, sometimes, the governing body as a whole into a closer working relationship with the staff employed at the school. Thus, at School 8, the head teacher referred to the Chair of governors giving a great deal of time to the school and has 'steered me and supported me in turning the school round. We have regular meetings. She is a great influence and a strong support, particularly in negotiating with the LEA.' He also refers to the confidence-building consequences of having a governor who is a partner in a major firm of consultants: 'She has given us confidence in dealing with LMS, particularly with no historical information from the LEA'.

The second main structural change is in the appointment of a new type of staff member. Many of the schools have appointed – or regraded – staff as bursars or finance managers. In none of the 15 schools are these appointments on a level comparable with the deputy head teachers and they seem to be in a service and support role. The potential difficulties with these appointments are encapsulated by interviews at School 13. The school's appointment of a financial manager followed extensive discussions between the head teacher and members of the governing body. Governors were concerned that the head teacher should not continue to be closely involved in financial administration but there was a concern that the post should not become influential because of control of budget information. The title of bursar was felt to carry the wrong messages, hence the choice of financial manager. We have also drawn attention to the appointment in School 8 of a property bursar and others, School 10 for example, have senior staff whose main duties are the premises.

Processes of decision making were described in the interviews and it was apparent that delegation had led to changes. We organise our account of these changes into five themes: financial information; control; planning; flexibility; and speed.

Decision making in these schools was often informed by better financial information. In School 1, a head of department reported that all department heads get a financial breakdown of the budget available for curriculum-related trips: 'This enables all departments to see where the money has gone throughout the school – this is more open and a good thing'. This openness does not appear to extend to all budget information, however, the same person commenting that 'Staff are not aware of what extra funds might be available, except for the basic capitation allowance'. The impact of more information is illustrated also by a decision to leave the LEA grounds maintenance contractors when the tender came up for renewal: receipt of other quotations made it apparent that the school could have the work done for much less money.

Delegation has also brought an awareness of greater control over resources on the part of some of those interviewed, School 9 providing an interesting illustration. The governing body of the school has used its employer position to prepare and implement a policy of staff attention, retention and motivation (ARM). It includes free food and coffee during working hours with medical insurance planned. The head teacher estimated that about £3,000 is spent currently on staff hospitality. A head of department in School 6 characterised the sense of control as entrepreneurial:

I consider myself something of a product of LMS. Being somewhat entrepreneurial by nature, I felt restricted by the limits of spending before LMS. Although not a budget holder in those distant days, it was a commonly held belief that the prescribed companies you could go to (*had* to go to) charged over the odds and gave poor service.

Contradictory views can be held about the greater sense of control arising from delegation. In School 10, one deputy commented 'post LM, I have the freedom to get on with things and decide what is wanted', but a head of department was not yet persuaded: 'I don't know if it's made any difference at all. When I ask for more teachers, I don't get it.' The Chair of the governing body, on the other hand, felt that 'LMS gives more breadth' than a pre-existing scheme of financial delegation.

Allied to a greater sense of control is the capacity to plan. A deputy head at School 5 linked these:

> the ability to have more control over resources has led to much improved use of resources and improved quality of forward planning.

A deputy head at School 8 observed that 'LMS has enabled us to plan ahead', referring to a rolling programme for improving the premises and the capacity to identify and plan for short term and long term develop-ment. School 10 is an example of planning where the senior staff are seeking to manage resources over a seven-year period. They are seeking to protect their sixth form curriculum over a period when pupil numbers are declining before a later increase. Their plan is to accumulate a surplus from the period of early buoyant enrolment and use this to meet the curriculum costs of the sixth form during the period of decline. The immediate consequence is a large surplus of £200,000. Whatever the merits of the case, it is an example which illustrates the entitlement of schools to make decisions based upon their own analysis of strategic priorities:

> Every year we say to potential sixth-formers – what do you want to study and we'll arrange it . . . . A demand-led economy may lead to two non-viable groups in the option blocks . . . . In 1992/93, ran French A-level group for four students. 1993/94 won't be much better but they will continue to be funded . . . for four years this will be done to meet the decline before growth. Doing this is what LMS is all about, not about managing for 2, 3, 6 months but for 2, 3, 6 years.

Knowing what is to be done and having the control to achieve objectives are linked with greater flexibility and the ability to get things done more quickly. Flexibility includes being able to carry funds over from one financial year to the next. It means being able to negotiate with commercial organisations and government agencies for matched funding of projects, a feature of activity in School 6, for example. It also means being able to arrange temporary contracts for staff more easily and teachers can also be recruited early. These comments are illustrative of the capacity to act more quickly as a result of not having to go through procedures established by the LEA. This benefit was reported by locally managed as well as grant maintained schools but it is a theme which allows us to conclude with some brief comments on the distinctive position of grant maintained schools with respect to decision making.

Decision making and grant maintained schools

GM schools are responsible for all aspects of provision, receiving enhanced funding to allow them to meet those responsibilities. It is germane to ask, therefore, whether and how these additional responsibilities and funding have affected ways of making decisions, as compared with their LM counterparts.

The head teacher and Chair of the governing body in School 13 were forceful in their expression of the benefits of GM for decision making. The head teacher remarked:

GM is perfect for me. It gives me the ability to develop and change at speed. In 1989, I advised against GM and two years later I decided that the LEA was a great millstone around the neck of the school.

This sense of greater opportunity was echoed by the Chair of the governing body:

LM gave us a little more flexibility but only managing what you were given. GM – with central government funding – we are able to have control of the money in the interests of the staff and pupils.

And by some other comments by the Head:

Although GM schools gain significant extra funding, I would prefer to be GM with less than LEA funding, rather than in the LEA with more than GM funding.

These comments on the added benefits of being a GM school show the opportunities provided for development. The autonomy and budgetary control of GM status give a capacity for flexible response which is not readily available to an LM school. These are also benefits cited by the head teacher in School 13. She observed that it was possible to earmark funds from the revenue budget for building after making due provision for those services which were no longer provided by the LEA.

Positive as these statements are about the wider scope of decisions at GM schools, they do not refer directly to any changes in the structures and processes of decision making as a result of the change. Indeed, in School 13, the head teacher observed that 'I don't see very much difference between LM and GM', other than in the amount of money available to the school. The latter was apparent in that the school was obtaining benefits through major building programmes, of which it had felt deprived as an LEA school.

Absence of direct evidence of change in the processes of decision making may obscure the indirect consequences of GM on these processes. Access to more resources does allow development – such as the provision of shower-room facilities for staff – which can have an indirect effect on their sense of well-being. Such feelings may contribute to staff views about the school and the concern of the school's management for their welfare. This can feed back positively into their participation in the school. Set against this were some concerns about isolation. One senior teacher noted that contact was being lost over curriculum developments in other schools. It is, she said, 'up to us to make the links and keep them going but you do get more isolated'.

Decision making is a theme to which we shall return in the later case studies and this will provide a further opportunity to examine any emerging differences between LM and GM schools. We now turn to consider the use to which the 15 schools have put their responsibilities over resources.

STAFFING FOR EFFECTIVENESS

All the schools we visited had used their delegated authority over staffing. Perhaps this is scarcely surprising in view of the importance of staff for schools and also because it uses such a large part of any school's budget. In providing examples of how schools have used their power over staffing, we have organised the material into two main sections. The first examines the use of delegated powers with respect to teaching staff. The second considers decisions concerned with staff who, by virtue of their work, give close support to the task of teaching and the provision of the curriculum.

Delegated budgets and teachers

Teachers to match needs

Many of those whom we interviewed made positive comments about the way delegated management allowed schools to make staffing decisions which matched their needs. Examples were given of changes – normally increases – to the complement of teachers above the level it would have been on the curriculum formula previously used by their LEA. School 6 reported that the two additional staff were used in a curriculum support role in the school. In School 8, 1.5 additional staff had been appointed and the casual employment of additional teachers for covering absent teachers was now rarely used. In School 3, the opportunity to improve the PTR (Pupil–Teacher Ratio) and have smaller groups had led to the 'better preparation and delivery of materials' with 'Teachers in a better psychological frame of mind when in front of the class' (deputy).

At School 13, it was decided to employ two additional teachers to assist with the development of information technology across the curriculum: 'one a subject specialist and the other an IT specialist' (head teacher). The appointment had contributed to cross-curricular work and 'staff, as well as pupils, had gained knowledge of IT'. The curriculum now better meets the needs and preferences of the pupils 'than some borough formula' and 'This means that by far the majority of girls get the subjects they choose which obviously leads to a better staff/student relationship' (deputy). At School 9, grant maintained status has allowed the appointment of many additional teachers, eight from the GM budget. This has allowed the school to respond to the preferences of teachers for 'more non-contact time whilst retaining small class sizes' (deputy).

An unusual example of employing teachers to match needs was re-ported by School 10. Projections of pupil numbers at this school showed a decline in pupil numbers before subsequently rising. It was decided to maintain the same curriculum over the period of decline: 'Governors accepted a staffing principle based upon the PTR in 1990. Management followed through that decision' (Head). When funds first increased as pupil numbers rose, the additional funds were set aside, to be drawn upon as numbers decline. These reserves are used principally to maintain a sixth form programme which is closely tailored to meet the preferences of the students.

At School 4, more teachers with skills in special needs have been employed and these worked across the school: 'special needs teachers are available now on an increasingly wide basis to meet the needs of children with learning difficulties – mainly in the lower school', as a result of which 'We have more effective mixed ability teaching' (head of history). At School 6, a decision had been made to double the amount of Drama in the curriculum and make the consequent staffing appointments.

Other schools also reported the employment of teachers with specialist subject skills. At School 1, the head teacher gave an account of a decision to employ an outreach teacher, an initiative previously blocked by the local authority. This was 'the most dramatic in-school and out-of-school de-velopment .... An outreach teacher was appointed and an outreach worker to develop links with families .... This has made the biggest difference to the way we work as a school.' Used to establish closer links with families and communities in a school with 90 per cent of the intake of Asian origin, the head teacher commented extensively on these benefits of the appointments:

I am told by subject teachers that there has been an immediately noticeable change in the way the school is seen by students and the way we are seen by parents, individually and at evening meetings .... We can deal immediately with all kinds of difficulties students have encountered to do with personal organisation and the curriculum. Where family support is assessed to be a potential problem the team has been directed to help .... calling a family conference and exploring futures acceptable to all. This is usually over 16+ and continuing studies beyond that age.

On homework, he remarked that 'this is now better understood and parents know better what is required'.

The opportunity to make appointments which meet perceived needs has one other dimension. In some schools, we were advised that it was now possible to move more quickly in advertising appointments and that this had led to better appointments. At School 13, an example was given of an early appointment made following the departure of a teacher in mid-year. The quickly appointed replacement allowed 'continuity and support to examination classes at a crucial time in the school year' (senior teacher).

Flexibility in deployment

Using the powers of delegation to employ staff to meet needs contributes to schools examining opportunities which were not previously open to them. The employment of the outreach teacher in School 1 is one such example. Delegation has, however, contributed to these schools looking afresh at their organisation and using their delegated powers to deploy staff in different ways.

The decision at School 3 to replace a departing deputy with a senior teacher appointment reflects this flexibility. The new appointment has been given responsibility for grounds, premises and marketing. More important, the head teacher argued that the wider restructuring of the management team motivated senior staff to review the 16+ curriculum, rethink the pastoral curriculum and focus on in-service provision.

At School 6, funding has been managed to allow more non-teaching time for heads of department. This has allowed staff to devote more time to links with primary schools as well as enabling more liaison within the school. At School 7, more time has been allocated for tutorials, as well as for departmental meetings to work on the implementation of action plans. One deputy commented that the 'change had facilitated structured action planning, particularly in Year 11, 12 and 13' and the extra time for tutorials has assisted work on Records of Achievement.

School 12 includes a continuing education facility and this is being managed increasingly as part of the whole provision. By treating the school and continuing education facility as one, it has been possible to develop a greater emphasis on tutorial-based teaching methods, giving a 'more adult feel to the school' (deputy head, community). More generally, it helped the school to avoid some redundancies by giving access to some financial reserves.

At School 14, the time of a teacher had been directed towards curriculum co-ordination with a brief for advising departments on the production of learning materials. The member of staff was given timetable contact with five departments during 1992–3 and the scheme as a whole received a positive evaluation by the LEA. Elsewhere, the deployment of staff has been accompanied by other changes and below we consider the use made of incentive allowances, fixed term contracts and staff development funds.

Pay, conditions and professional development

Staff interviewed in about half the schools gave accounts of the use of incentive allowances to support new developments, including substantial restructuring of responsibilities. At School 6, a higher allowance was made available when the post of head of modern languages was advertised and the head teacher was anxious 'to get a good quality response'. The result had included an increase in foreign trips and in entries to Key Stage 4 'but results are shaky so far'. The head of science was asked on appointment to prepare a Development Plan for the department: 'We created a clearly defined Second in Science with responsibility for KS3 on a B allowance and one staff member was made responsible for KS4 with an A allowance. These were both new allowances created for existing members of staff' (head of science). He went on to comment that the 'National Curriculum has meant great changes at this school. There was no KS3 in place – only on paper. Time was a premium.' The new responsibilities and the use of technician support – see below – are contributing to meeting the challenge.

School 9 reports major developments in the use of incentive allowances. As a locally managed school, 65 per cent of staff received an allowance, a figure which has gone up to 89 per cent since the school became grant maintained. It also supports its staff with an 'Attention, retention and motivation' (ARM) policy 'which includes free food/coffee during working hours and will include medical insurance from next year. I reckon we spend up to £3000 pa on staff hospitality' (Head).

At School 14, incentive allowances have been used as part of a policy to develop curriculum differentiation. A teacher has been given an 'A' allowance to work with staff and to advise them on the development of strategies and design of teaching materials for the delivery of the National Curriculum. In assessing its impact, a deputy remarked: 'Obviously the rate of development will be different from area to area. People have made progress in terms of resourcing and in terms of sensitivity.'

A final example from School 10 shows how allowances are being used flexibly. In order to encourage more application of IT, 'A' allowances or their equivalent are being allocated to six departments. This succeeds the previous year's policy when time was allowed but little was done, possibly because the person was not the most suitable for the task. This use of time-limited allowances has been taken further in School 7, where some staff have been employed on fixed term contracts. This applied to the head of mathematics, for example, who commented that it 'does focus your mind to produce the "goods" in the time. I must justify what I have done.'

Authority over funds for professional development was mentioned in at least five schools. At School 16, much of the staff development budget is devolved to departments who can use the budget how they want, whether to buy time for cover or go out for training. The Head's assessment of the policy is that 'teachers feel better equipped to deal with the National Curriculum'. It has been possible, he suggested, to plan Programmes of Study, to examine differentiated learning strategies and to review reporting and assessment. School 10 has made substantial additions from its local management budget to the base staff development allocation. £25,000 has been added to the specific allocation of training funds. Some of this has been used in association with a university to examine methodologies of teaching. Commenting on this initiative, the Chair of governors observed that 'teachers were learning more of the methodologies' and the commitment to each other was assisting its development as a project with benefit for the school.

Comments elsewhere drew attention to the need to be able to involve support staff in professional development. Examples of their involvement and their effect on schools are the theme of the next section.

Support staff and the curriculum

Innovative uses of support staff in schools have recently been examined in a study for the DFEE (Mortimore and Mortimore with Thomas 1994). That report recognised the way in which schools were reviewing the employment and deployment of staff so that there was a better match between the qualifications and cost of staff and their role in schools. This notion of fitness-for-purpose is a development which might be expected from delegated management and it is, therefore, not surprising that we encounter developments in the use of support staff in our set of good practice schools.

In the account which follows, we have organised the cases we report into two broad categories. In the first of these we consider examples where schools have identified a need for a person, with a particular set of skills, who is required to improve the curriculum provided at the school. These needs may be available from teachers but, more typically, they are to be found in another skilled and qualified occupation. In effect, without these people, certain curriculum development would have been unlikely to have occurred. In the second category, we consider cases where tasks could be done by teachers, as with photocopying, but they are more efficiently done by someone else who is likely to be suitably trained and, moreover, costs less than teachers. We should observe that this division is not absolute and there will be cases which could be located in either section.

Curriculum-led expertise

Appointments of specialists in information technology (IT) and in librarian work typify a number of the appointments made in the 15 schools we visited. Schools have also increased the number of laboratory and reprographic technicians on their staff.

Five schools have appointed librarians, some of whom have Chartered Librarian status. School 4 has undertaken a major reorganisation of its library facilities, previously in three locations. These are now on one site with a member of staff in charge of resources, assisted by one librarian and three assistants: 'The impetus for a resource base was driven by National Curriculum project work and for early GCSE – we wanted to provide resources for that' (Head). School 8 has also appointed a professional librarian. The head of history commented that the appointment means 'Children can now do research assignments with qualified help – this provides equality of opportunity for children, not just those whose parents can help outside school'.

The same school has appointed a reprographics technician: 'The biggest improvement has been reprographics. The previous system was dreadful' (head of history). He went on to observe that 'The National Curriculum is based upon worksheets. Reprographics support helps with this – makes it easier to set homework. There is no need for extensive notes; we teach the curriculum through worksheets which makes it much easier and efficient.'

At School 6, the head of science has been able to increase technician support from one to two, although half of the extra is shared with the mathematics department. The additional support has allowed the department 'to develop the practical side of the curriculum'. Since the preparation for practicals is done by the technicians, it has released 'teaching time for teachers and relieved stress'.

School 12 has made several appointments in these areas, including a Chartered Librarian, an IT technician and a resource assistant. The head teacher expressed the view that these appointments had made a major contribution to the school's flexible learning project. IT support has also been introduced in a number of the other schools visited. At School 1, this support is based in the lower school and is all the more useful because the member of staff is based in the library; he also does undertake a number of small maintenance tasks. The appointment has helped with 'the smooth running of the lab. and the use of resources such as the video' (deputy). He goes on to suggest that the benefits are increased use of the video and a better standard of materials for pupils, who receive newly printed worksheets more often. In School 10, the IT support and the wider investment in that area is regarded as 'fundamental' by the Head who sees this resource as contributing to staff and pupil development.

There are cases of schools reporting the employment of additional support staff to work alongside teachers in classrooms. In School 3, classroom support is provided for teachers in the maths department through assistance from a special needs ancillary worker. This development has 'enabled weaker groups to progress at a greater rate by giving each pupil needing support more one-to-one contact' (head of mathematics). The maths department at School 4 also uses classroom assistants: 'An increased need for learning support had been identified' (head of mathematics). While there was some concern at the lack of teachers, there was a recognition that this arrangement could work. The head of department concluded with the view: 'We are helping the less able to have a more satisfactory learning experience and we can stretch the most able. It helps with differentiation. We are using the support assistants to stretch the most able at the moment.'

Efficient substitution

Delegated management offers the opportunity for schools to audit their use of staff and match skills to people in ways which secure effective performance at the lowest reasonable cost. The final typing and preparation of material for pupils is an example of work which is often done by teachers but could often be done to a higher standard and more quickly by suitably trained clerical and secretarial staff. Schools 4, 5, 9, 12 and 13 all report examples where the use of teacher time in this activity has been replaced with clerical support.

At School 5, office staff have been encouraged by the head teacher to understand their role in terms of supporting the work of teachers. The support team in the office were reorganised to meet new demands and the result is 'A more defined structure' within which staff 'can work more quickly' and helps in the preparation of 'bespoke differentiated materials – we have rapidity of response' (Head). At School 4, the establishment of clerical support has been increased by 25 per cent and now stands at two term-time only staff at 25 hours per week and an increase from part-time secretaries to two full-time. The benefits of this support were summarised by the head of geography at School 12. On typing materials for curriculum use, she reported that 'one person gives us continuity, improved presentation and a departmental style is developing'. It has 'led us to think in detail about content of material and include evaluations for students, to consider our approaches'. Such substitution has also occurred elsewhere, as in the reorganisation of administrative systems in schools.

ADMINISTRATION AND INFRASTRUCTURE

All schools need administrative staff and systems to support their work. Delegation increased the administrative demands upon schools but also gave them an opportunity to match resources to needs in these areas of activity. This is an area where it is difficult to explain the benefits of change in terms of any effect upon the processes of teaching and learning in a school. We did, nonetheless, ask this question and received interesting and relevant replies. The account is in two main sections, beginning with the introduction of technology-based systems designed to facilitate adminis-tration. We include in this account information on one of a small number of schools which have made substantial structural changes to their adminis-trative support system. This is followed by a section which describes the different personnel appointed to contribute to school administration, including appointments concerned with property administration.

System management

More than ten schools reported the introduction of computerised manage-ment information systems. Undoubtedly, these are a smaller number than actually have such systems but chose not to mention them in our interviews. These systems, of which SIMS was frequently mentioned, provided facilities for resource management as well as helping with other aspects of school administration.

In School 3, the head of mathematics reported the appointment of an office ancillary to have responsibility for pupil records and reporting, and the purchase of software to enable profiling to be introduced. His assess-ment of the value of this change was that 'with our assessments directly linked to pupil profiles, pupils and parents have a better understanding of what has been taught'. The head of humanities was also the examina-tions officer and explained how their system had allowed him to produce, for all pupils, 'an examination plan/profile, including a seating plan. The system will also give us the results and be used for analysis.' This school was one of a small number which reported a major restructuring of their administrative/support system. Appointments include: an assistant bur-sar; information officer; school nurse; cover for holiday periods; and extended secretarial help through to 5 o'clock each day. Benefits of these changes include: 'All data relating to students now effectively managed and recorded and more effective "tracking" of the use of resources to the benefit of all' (Head).

At School 4, the SIMS system means 'many jobs can be done more quickly and efficiently. It also provides better information, for example, with the timetable. It gives us reasonable oversight of budgetary control, pupil records of attainment and pupil assessment' (Head). As to its effect on learning and teaching, the main reported benefit was the release of senior staff time to oversee the implementation of the National Curriculum.

Uncertainty about the effect of management information systems on learning was evident at School 5. The SIMS system records all financial information and pupil records at the school. The head teacher was unwilling to suggest that this had an impact on teaching and learning, however, commenting that 'I feel uneasy about schools who make such claims'. Although he did recognise that technology-based systems do allow a more rapid and flexible response and can free teacher time, he observed that the deputy still spends a lot of time on administration. Set against these anxieties are the views of the head of mathematics and the head of modern languages. The former referred to the new systems: 'Improved support for teachers. Improved record-keeping facility – you can get it done quicker; speedier retrieval.' The head of modern languages was also the co-ordinator for Records of Achievement and cited the role of office staff in entering these data using word processors. Pupils benefit because records are available in time of college interviews: 'This means we can send out our pupils for interview with well presented RoAs'.

The quality of these systems depends upon several factors, not least the people who are responsible for them and the management of the administrative system. The role of these staff, as well as others working in school administration, is examined below.

People in administration

From almost all the schools we received examples of new appointments or extra hours for administration. The roles and titles of these people were often diverse, although it was sometimes the case that titles differed but roles were similar.

Office staff appointments included finance officers and finance secretaries, bursars, examinations officers and managers. At School 8, a finance officer was previously a head of physics. He has retained a teaching role but is no longer a head of department. Working with the support of a secretary 'he does anything related to finance' and, together, 'they have freed up the Head's time' (Chair of governors). Commenting on the benefits of this post, the head of history remarked that: 'There are now no deadlines for spending money. We used to have to make instant decisions but now we can take time to consider decisions and choose the best materials from the publishers. Immediate needs can also be met.' The school has created the post of property bursar who has an estates manager with 'handyman skills'.

School 9 has a more extensive and revised administrative structure. At this grant maintained school, there is a personnel co-ordinator, a technical services manager, a salaries clerk acting as a payroll officer, a registrar and other secretarial and clerical support. The school now has between one-third and one-half more support staff and functions have been transferred to these staff from the deputy heads. The head of maths described some of the consequences: 'I don't have to spend time doing administration and can spend time teaching, meeting and discussing with the maths team. This facilitates better delivery of the maths curriculum and pastoral curriculum through the team.'

Viewed as a set, our interviews show that the importance of a sound administrative structure is well understood. As with other studies of delegated management, there is clear evidence of additional resources being provided for this part of work in schools. It is also an area where suitably qualified and lower paid staff are doing tasks previously, and inappropriately, done by more senior staff. Important cost and efficiency savings can be gained through such changes.

Describing any direct relationship between administration and the quality of teaching and learning is not easy. A number of those interviewed, however, drew attention to circumstances where the consequences for teachers and pupils were very direct: improving pupil reporting systems and allowing orders for learning materials to be processed quickly.

AN ENVIRONMENT FOR LEARNING

All schools in the study have taken the opportunity presented by delegated management to adapt and improve the fabric of the buildings and to enhance facilities for both staff and students. 'Locally determined use of space' – as described in School 12 – was clearly seen as a tangible benefit in the context of school-based decision making. A number of school buildings have been neglected over past years. Several of them were enjoying the benefits of local authority capital building projects, either with the aim of bringing the school onto one site from a split site, or in response to increasing rolls over recent years. In all cases, grant maintained schools had benefited from further capital funding or had applied to do so in the coming year.

> A lot of money has gone into the school environment – GM money has made a difference – you get a feeling of a pleasant working environment. The improved working environment has made a difference to the ethos of the school and the attitude of pupils.
>
> (deputy head, School 9)

The opportunity to improve the standard of the school environment generally and thus enhance the physical conditions for teaching and learning for both staff and pupils is significant.

> Greater flexibility in handling premises budget brings general benefits which come from higher morale and a feeling that 'the system' is more

responsive. This is also all part of a general concern to improve pupils' awareness of and concern for the environment.

(deputy head, School 4)

In the majority of cases decisions over use of premises were curriculum led. Four schools had a rolling programme of adapting premises into curriculum area suites. Often the shape of the programme would be influenced by National Curriculum subjects as they came 'on stream' – six schools had programmes of refurbishment of science facilities. The provision of other facilities would be in response to National Curriculum demands, particularly those which might also prove to have tangible, marketable qualities, for example technology rooms or music suites. A majority of schools had improved their library and resources provision in response to increased emphasis in the curriculum for individual research skills and project-based work. The availability of external grants targeted at particular curriculum areas was clearly a contributory factor.

In several instances schools had taken the decision to employ their own site managers usually with the capability of carrying out minor repairs in-house. Some had given managerial responsibility for premises to an existing member of the teaching staff. Such examples have already been explored under staffing issues. There were a few examples of schools which had decided to employ their preferred contractors for grounds maintenance, cleaning, catering or other premises services.

Four primary categories have emerged from the data which are reported on as follows: reorganisation into curriculum suites; refurbishment of teaching rooms and public areas; information technology across the curriculum; library and resource bases.

Reorganisation into curriculum suites

Curriculum suiting across the school

Two of the schools in the study had initiated a programme of premises reorganisation to facilitate curriculum suiting. Both were on large sites, one was a split site linked by footbridge and the other comprised two main buildings albeit on the same campus. Both schools needed to remodel old-style buildings which were in poor repair. School 6 had been able to complete extensive internal premises alterations with the inclusion of a small cluster of computers housed in each curriculum area, thus bringing information technology into easy access for all subjects. This was a result of a rolling programme based on National Curriculum subjects as they came on stream, and the benefit of a good deal of external matched funding. Together with a programme of refurbishment for each curriculum area, the impact of such reorganisation of premises provided the catalyst in motivating and rejuvenating a 'disenchanted staff' – most of whom had taught in the school for many years – and giving them a sense of identity and purpose. The head of the science department, for example, where a new science laboratory had been created plus the renovation of an old one, was also making use of his capitation budget to save for 'extras' such as a departmental computer for staff use. This was to enable record keeping of department stocks and easy access to pupil records and National Curriculum assessments. The department had initiated the practice of displaying pupil results on the departmental notice board which the head of department described as: 'the single most motivating factor for pupils I have ever seen'. He also claimed that: 'The ethos of the whole department has changed. I am convinced this [improved environment] affects the attitude of the pupils and the staff.'

Curriculum suiting for departments

Two schools had particularly targeted craft, design and technology (CDT). School 8 remodelled an existing block in order to bring this area of the curriculum into one building as part of the school policy to correct a perceived weakness. A new head of department was appointed, on the retirement of the former head, with particular experience of control technology and a £200,000 award from the Technology Schools Initiative was used to fund new equipment. Former art rooms, woodwork and metalwork areas were adapted and refurbished and the existing toilet block reduced in size to make space for a larger resources area. Funding for the enterprise came from various sources: TVEI funding of £5,000; Local Education Authority funding of £5,000; a sponsored walk by pupils of £2,000; a generous £91,000 from a local charity; and £3,000 from school budget. The school recognised that such a development would enable high quality delivery of the CDT curriculum in line with National Curriculum requirements. School 16 also brought together elements of the CDT curriculum, such as home economics and art, into a new block when an LEA capital building project presented the opportunity. The enhanced environment, increased space and upgraded facilities enable the school to offer a wide range of technology courses: 'Pupils are increasingly taking up options in textiles, art and graphics.'

Just under half of the schools had programmes of refurbishment to science laboratories. The funding for one school was made possible by GM capital funding for a new technology block, a second school had a new block funded by the local authority and a third was now benefiting from the facilities of nine laboratories. Improved facilities for practical science were clearly an issue. One school described the improvements as 'bringing the environment into the 1990s'. Enhanced science facilities were felt by another school to help to attract good quality teachers and were enabling the school to deliver a modular science curriculum.

Schools 1, 5 and 9 had developed new music suites. School 9 had provided a music technology studio adjacent to practice rooms. A new director of music had been appointed on a flexible contract with a low teaching timetable in order to develop extra curricular music. School 5 was still in the process of developing a music suite by adapting existing premises. The Parent–Teacher Association was raising funds to provide instruments. The school hoped to develop extra curricular musical tuition, not only for pupils, but also for members of the local community, on a self-financing basis.

Refurbishment of teaching rooms and public areas

All schools in the study had decided to allocate funds to general refurbishment of the school environment. Several had a rolling programme phased over some years in which to redecorate systematically and refurbish where necessary throughout the school. The Head of School 9 told us:

> We have our own five year plan to decorate, remodel and refurbish our school to provide a civilised environment. The money for this sort of thing never reached the school before. This will result in better exam results, higher staying on rates, more national awards, better behaviour.

All the schools acknowledged the civilising and motivating impact which the environment had on staff and students alike. 'If the environment is good you give 2% more', one head of department told us. A Head felt: 'Children respond to a quality environment'. Another head of department said: 'The quality of the environment is important and a stimulus for learning.'

Many schools have improved their teaching rooms, often with carpeting, sometimes with window blinds. As was commented in School 10: 'An enhanced classroom environment enhances the learning process.' In School 6 refurbishment of the history and geography suites had created a more pleasant working environment, valued and respected by staff and pupils alike: 'I have noticed a recognisable effect on the pupils' (head of history).

The widest brief was adopted in adapting premises. Public areas had been decorated in several schools, not least due to a recognition of the importance of the image of the school for visitors and the significance of a welcoming and pleasant atmosphere. Increased emphasis on staff and student facilities was also evident in some schools, highlighting the value of personnel and their working conditions. Schools which were involved in reorganisation into curriculum suites usually tried to incorporate offices for departmental heads.

Information technology across the curriculum

All schools in the study have enhanced their capability to deliver information technology across the curriculum. Premises have been adapted to include the provision of 'bookable' computer suites, model offices or smaller 'nests' or 'clusters' of computers in curriculum areas. Technology is thus more accessible throughout the curriculum, as a cross-curricular theme and also for flexible resource-based learning by individual students.

The availability and accessibility of computing equipment to support the delivery of information technology across the curriculum has clearly been a high priority for schools. Indeed, in most schools this has been identified as an area of greatest need for new equipment in order to meet National Curriculum requirements. Such extra resourcing, however, does have significant funding implications and several schools in the study have drawn upon various sources of external funding. Often this has resulted in the schools benefiting from the most up to date technology and a higher number of computers per pupil than might otherwise have been possible. It is clear that effective delivery of information technology throughout the curriculum requires efficient organisation of easy and equitable access to good quality equipment. Many schools have also upgraded their library resources to include information technology and this aspect will be further explored in the following section.

Technology suites

School 3 had collaborated with a computer company to help equip a multimedia learning centre adjacent to an information technology room and computer equipped language centre. This was part of a policy to upgrade learning resource facilities within the school and to encourage the use of video and word processing as part of flexible learning.

School 5 partly attributed improved examination results in GCSE technology to the creation of two computer suites in the school and planned a further suite to be operational from Easter 1993. These rooms are bookable and under the supervision of an IT co-ordinator, to ensure that all pupils have access. Here again, the school recognised the resulting possibilities of freeing up their existing hardware for use elsewhere in curriculum areas. The school also acknowledged the marketable qualities of such facilities to prospective parents: 'Computer suites are a tangible showpiece – computers have a high profile with parents.'

Computer 'clusters' in curriculum areas

Three schools had chosen to develop clusters of computers in curriculum areas as part of their policy to increase provision of information technology.

School 16 had spent £100,000 from school budget over the last two years establishing fully equipped computer 'nests' in six of its curriculum areas. This was as a result of a decision to move away from a central bookable computer suite. The curriculum areas now had at least six Archimedes computers which were networked. The maths department, for example, has its own cluster of networked computers with computer points in every teaching room and four trolleys to move machines around as necessary. In the history department more information technology software was being used to facilitate different teaching methods and easier differentiation of learning styles for individual pupils. Word processing skills also help to boost the morale of slow learners and increase the possibilities of their presentation skills. A member of staff in the department acknowledged, 'It extends our options for teaching and learning styles.'

School 6 adopted a whole school plan to include clusters of computers in each curriculum area as the school was reorganised into curriculum suites. Matched funding from external sources had helped to facilitate this. The humanities suite had two computers funded with TVI money with two printers funded from the school's special initiative fund. This facility has been developed into an open access resource area for flexible learning projects and the new technology is used for information technology within the humanities curriculum – as a bookable teaching room. Thus the new technology is more accessible to pupils not only in class time but in free time also for research projects and homework. The head of history acknowledged that the cluster of computers within the faculty was having the effect that the information technology elements of the curriculum were being better delivered. A commercial arrangement between the school and a computer manufacturer had been set up. In exchange for the school being used as a regional information centre for the company – a 'shop window for the use of computers in education' – the company had provided in the region of £22,000 worth of equipment. Thus the school has the benefit of the latest equipment in a customised technology suite. As a result of this, equipment which had formerly been used in the technology department was distributed to other areas of the curriculum. External sources of funding had also been used by School 17 to increase its equipment capacity by establishing model office suites.

Library and resource bases

Whole school resource bases

Eight of the schools in the study had developed their library resource facilities and several had incorporated resources for information technology provision. While departmental resource bases were often also targeted, the redevelopment of whole school resources provision often provided the opportunity to bring other support services for staff together into one area, such as reprographics, with enhanced ancillary staffing to enable staff to make full use of the resources available.

School 4 had addressed the issue of whole school library provision. A new lower school building funded by the LEA had presented the opportunity to create a physical base for whole school resource provision. Some TVI money had been used initially to stock the library and 10 per cent of each department's capitation budget was allocated for ongoing resourcing. Previously the school had operated three separate libraries run by the English department. The new facility is supervised by a member of the teaching staff who is assisted by a full-time librarian and three administrative assistants. The school felt that in this way it was addressing some parental concern which had been expressed over lack of resources and would provide adequate resources for GCSE project work.

Six other schools had put extra funds into library provision. External funding was a common factor in enabling such projects. School 5 used TVI funding to employ a librarian for its redeveloped whole school resource centre and parents' contributions of £15,000 funded materials and equipment. The decision to redevelop the library was described by the school as being 'at the core of changes in teaching and learning styles, a move towards independent learning and an encouragement to staff to use the centre in lesson time and for pupils' homework and extra-curricular activities'. Learning material support was also concentrated in the same area – reprographics, audio-visual aids – and a member of staff was appointed as head of resources on a 'D' allowance to supervise and co-ordinate.

School 3 remodelled an existing area and developed a multimedia learning centre which incorporated adjacent information technology rooms and language centre. Collaborative funding enabled the development: £20,000 from school budget, £10,000 from a parents' covenant scheme and computing equipment donated by a computer manufacturer. The previous school library had been for the sixth form and was staffed by a teacher-librarian. The school now employs a learning centre manager who has a low teaching commitment in order to devote more time to pupils in the study centre. The new facility is an important part of the school's flexible learning programme and enables teachers to 'support and direct but pupils take responsibility for their own learning' (deputy head).

A full-time professional librarian is now employed from the school budget in School 8 to supervise an extended and restocked library. Funds from the school budget together with £18,000 from local charities were used to purchase learning materials and TVI money had been used to refurbish a sixth form study room. The Senior Management Team in School 16 identified the library as a weak area and the school's Resource Management Committee found funds to remedy this. As a result the library area was extended, refurbished and restocked. A Chartered Librarian was appointed, initially half funded by the school and half funded by the Local Education Authority (LEA), but now wholly funded by the school. The Parent–Teacher Association (PTA) contributed funds for a library computer and encyclopaedias. A parent governor commented that his two children at the school had commented on the improved facility and were using it increasingly in free time.

In some schools departmental resource bases were being developed, as in School 7. Two schools were developing sixth form resource areas and four schools were targeting funds to establish or enhance careers libraries.

Enhancing the learning environment has clearly been an important priority for schools under delegated management. Funding curriculum materials and equipment is, however, no lesser a concern. The following section investigates developments in resource allocation in this area.

CURRICULUM MATERIALS

School expenditure on materials for the curriculum is an area which appears to have changed the least, procedurally, as a result of the impact of local management. Historically, schools have organised their spending on books and equipment through departmental budgets which have been allocated to heads of department by the head teacher. This has traditionally been known as the capitation budget. In general it should be noted that funding for learning materials has increased in the schools in the study. This includes extra funding, on a whole school basis, for curriculum initiatives and development, often in line with National Curriculum requirements. A clear link was expressed between the provision of adequate learning materials and the effective delivery of the curriculum. Commenting upon the provision of new materials for his school's technology department, the Chair of governors summed up this link: 'If money had not been made available then pupils would have been at a disadvantage – not sharing books is important and inadequate materials affects the learning process.'

The following sections draw upon evidence which suggests that resources for curriculum materials may be organised under three broad headings: departmental capitation funding; curriculum initiative and development; in-house materials.

Departmental capitation funding

'Formula funded' system

The trend in funding departmental learning materials appears to be towards a 'formula' funded system based upon pupil numbers and timetable sessions for each subject, usually with a weighting allowance for practical subjects, such as science, which require increased funding for consumables. Such a system is perceived to be more equitable for allocating a basic allowance to each curriculum area. In School 17 for example, this was perceived as a more effective process by which staff can see how decisions on budgets are reached. Alongside this, many of the schools in the study had a separate fund into which departments could bid for extra funding for curriculum development. Many schools had increased their funding for learning materials: School 3 had increased the funding by 12 per cent per annum and School 6 had increased the total amount by 50 per cent.

Local management had created an environment in which departmental and faculty heads could exercise much greater control over their budget. The relaxation of regulations which had previously tied schools to recommended local authority suppliers was commented upon several times. The new freedom to choose and purchase learning materials from other sources was resulting in better value for money and involving teachers more closely in purchasing decisions. 'We now have the flexibility to plan for the department's spending. Attitudes to spending have changed and the departmental staff are making their own choices' (head of science).

The head of science in School 1 commented on the ease and speed with which the department can buy small items of equipment from petty cash. He felt this was having a direct beneficial effect on the delivery of the science curriculum because staff would not put off doing certain things with a class because of lack of equipment. He also felt that: 'Better value for money enables us to provide more equipment for curriculum delivery.' In School 6 the science department had begun to keep computer stock records of consumables and a priority list of items to purchase. Whereas prior to local management the department had tended to hoard stocks, now these had been run down – which had released hundreds of pounds – and through careful use of the budget extra equipment had been purchased for special needs children.

Needs-based system

Other schools were developing a needs-based system establishing whole school priorities for funding learning materials. In School 5 each head of faculty made his or her case for the departmental budget requirements. This bid had to be based on curriculum need and justified in full. The process then required all information to be circulated prior to a meeting of all faculty heads at which the bids would be decided. The result of such a process is that some faculties would be more successful than others in 'winning' their funding. However, it was strongly felt that such an arrangement provided optimum use of the budget and it was accepted by staff that other faculties might have more pressing curriculum needs and that their own needs would be met appropriately. Such a needs-based system tended to follow National Curriculum demands.

School 14 also organised a bid system. However, more of the school's budget was delegated to the departments and the type of bid therefore needed to be more comprehensive. This included consumables, including reprographics, curriculum maintenance and development, any special curriculum activities, ancillary support and furniture repairs. Each department was also required to forecast the future trend anticipated for three years ahead in order to give senior management a base from which to plan. The aim of this more comprehensive system of departmental budgeting was to help to integrate the pastoral year groups, the site and curriculum management through curriculum teams occupying particular suites and being responsible for the pastoral care of a year group. It was also hoped to enable staff development as middle management assume a broader delegated role. Thus local management is not seen exclusively as a task for the senior management team and staff start to focus on the costs of classroom practice as a whole. While staff clearly understood the process, 'I see the capitation bids very firmly linked with departmental development plans as driven by the national curriculum' (head of history), in practice the school was not able to fund sufficient learning materials, which was commented on as a restraining factor: 'We never expected to have more money.' Indeed a lack of books for two year groups for history was putting a strain on the budget for reprographics. However, senior management remained realistic about the limitations of delegated management: 'We must be careful not to raise expectations too much – LMS does this. It's wonderful to own your own home providing you can pay the mortgage' (deputy head).

Curriculum initiatives and curriculum development

Many schools were providing funding over and above normal capitation requirements for curriculum innovation and development. Often such funding was allocated to departments in response to National Curriculum requirements for new learning materials and equipment. In most cases departments were required to put their case for extra funding from a curriculum initiative fund based on curriculum needs.

Targeted funding for curriculum initiative

School 7 had used some 'development money' to introduce Italian as a second modern language from Year 7 as an alternative to French. This would have the effect of broadening the modern languages curriculum offered by the school and give the opportunity for some students to study two modern languages higher up the school. Such increased provision required extra funding for appropriate learning materials and extra staffing.

School 7 had also provided extra funds of £1,400 for Year 7 and Year 8 history to initiate new National Curriculum courses. £1,000 had also been made available for a new head of history to develop the curriculum materials throughout the department and the Year 9 course had been changed and some new approaches had been initiated in the GCSE courses. A new A-level history course had also been funded. Such changes had only been made possible owing to the increased funding for materials together with departmental staffing changes. The head of history felt that as a result pupils were responding more positively to the subject, as teaching styles were developing, and the generally higher quality of learning materials was having a positive impact on learning: 'High quality accessible resources must bring about an improvement in learning.'

Curriculum support budget

School 10 had allocated additional funding of £25,000 and £15,000 from the school budget in addition to the departmental budget for National Curriculum resources. An example of the use of this was the provision of balanced science which had been reorganised within the school into a modular system. £7,000 of the extra funding had also been targeted at the humanities faculty for National Curriculum resources for history and geography.

School 16 operates a bid system for departmental budgets which includes curriculum development. Resource implications generated by departmental development plans would then be put forward for consideration. As an example of this the history department had bid for £1,000 for three years for KS3 as a rolling programme to equip the department with appropriate resources for the National Curriculum. The same department had also successfully bid for TVEI funding for learning materials required for a flexible learning project developed by the head of department. The school assessed all bids for learning materials against curriculum needs with the objective that 'children's learning is the highest priority'.

Through use of additional curriculum support moneys several schools had provided new or enhanced A-level courses.

Curriculum incentive payment for newly appointed heads of department

Three schools allocated lump sums to newly appointed heads of department to resource their departments. School 9 allocated £10,000 to a new head of maths. This was spent on books and basic equipment. School 7 allocated £1,000 to a new head of history (at the same time as refurbishing a teaching room in the humanities area as a resource base). Together with increased curriculum development funding, as described earlier, School 7 had thus begun to deliver the new National Curriculum course throughout the school in history. School 5 had decided to allocate £10,000 to a newly appointed head of department for special needs who was about to take up the post.

In-house materials

An interesting development in the context of local management is the emphasis placed on the production of in-house learning materials. As indicated above some schools have taken the opportunity to bring together support services in school into whole school resource bases. With this in mind some schools have appointed further ancillary staff or reprographic support or technicians to facilitate accessibility for teaching staff to different types of learning materials such as audio-visual aids. This issue of increased ancillary support has been more fully explored in the chapter on staffing.

Reprographics facilities

Clearly schools are aware of the importance of good quality reprographics facilities in the production of in-house learning materials. As mentioned above, School 5 provides a good example of where reprographics has been incorporated in redeveloped resources provision with extra ancillary staffing and a new responsibility for head of resources to an existing member of the teaching staff. Another school had targeted funds for reprographics support, both for equipment and staffing. A good example of the way in which the school is using the improved support is that all departments are asked to produce their own revision packs for Year 11 examination pupils. This is felt to provide practical assistance for pupils with the result of making them more effective and raising standards. Moreover, despite the improvement in the number of text books provided, gaps in learning materials still existed. The head of humanities commented on the importance of good quality in-house reprographics to enable the department to fill those gaps adequately. Thus, good quality differentiated materials could be used, particularly for the less able for whom standard texts were not always pitched at quite the right level. He felt that good quality in-house materials were 'bound to have an effect on raising standards'.

Funding staff time

Some schools are using their increased responsibilities over resources to fund staff time for the development of curriculum projects and learning materials. School 7 has funded time for staff within the maths department to test new curriculum materials and pilot them in class. This has enabled development of an individualised learning programme. School 3 delegated its training budget to each department which was used mainly for supply cover to give staff time for appropriate training. The history department of School 16 used TVI funds for learning materials to initiate a flexible learning project devised and developed within the department. As a result the department now has a full set of nineteenth century history books for use in the library. More importantly, perhaps, was the significance attached to this in-house development in generating a feeling of ownership of the project within the department and the positive response judged to have been received from pupils to the materials.

Differentiated materials

A whole school initiative in School 14 had been funded to buy staff time to work on differentiation in the curriculum. If funds can be maintained it is hoped to develop the initiative into a rolling programme in each curriculum area. The enhancement of learning was one of the targets of the School Development Plan and the project began with a training day launch for all staff. During the academic year 1992–3 a total of 12 teacher periods per week have been bought for curriculum development and a responsibility allowance has been awarded to a project co-ordinator to advise on the production of learning materials in support of differentiation strategies. The effectiveness of the project has already been reviewed by local authority advisers who observed 71 lessons in all subjects across Years 7–9. They judged the lessons 'to demonstrate a high degree of differentiation' through various approaches. The differentiation policy also involved learning strategies for special needs pupils and an able student project. The inspectors recognised 'the amount of work the curriculum areas have done to achieve the levels of differentiation ... and ... the considerable efforts made show excellent practice'.

Resources for curriculum materials are generally allocated from the school budget. However, curriculum delivery can also often be enhanced through collaboration with external providers. While many of these opportunities presented themselves prior to local management, the context of increased school autonomy is one which some schools are using to maximum effect. External sources of support are considered in the final section of this chapter on resource management.

EXTERNAL RELATIONS AND SUPPORT

Local management has made schools more aware of their external environment and the possibilities for collaboration and mutual support between schools and various external agencies. Working in partnership with the wider community can bring many benefits for schools, in terms of both financial and non-financial support. Some such arrangements are not new. Effective schools have always sought to work with parents, local commerce and industry and the LEA in a variety of ways. However, one result of increased school autonomy is the extent to which schools are adopting a much more entrepreneurial approach to seeking out external sources of funding and expertise. Many schools in the study gave us examples of how a 'bid' economy was being used to good effect as they attracted extra funding from central government initiatives, other government sponsored local agencies or commercial organisations. The increased use of school premises to provide services and facilities to the local community was also much in evidence and apparently working to mutual benefit. Evidence from the study suggests that external support, both financial and non-financial, comes largely from five sources, each of which is discussed in the following sections.

Local community

Schools' links with their local community often found a basis in mutual interest and resulted in mutual benefit. Such links varied, however, according to the location of the school and the support which the local community was able to give. In different circumstances it was sometimes more the case of what the school could offer the local community, rather than what the local community was able to offer the school by way of external resources.

Parent–Teacher Associations (PTAs)

PTAs which exist in many schools have often been one of the main sources of external funds for schools prior to local management. Our evidence shows that such support continues under delegated management. In several schools parents generated funds for the school through PTAs.

Four schools referred to substantial financial contributions to new developments from the PTA. School 3 funded books for the redeveloped library with £10,000 from a parents' covenant scheme. School 5 also made use of parents' contributions totalling £5,000 towards a new library and the PTA was in the process of raising funds for musical instruments to be used for after-school music club tuition. The Parents, Teachers and Friends Association of School 16 provided £7,000 for a library security system and bought a library computer for £1,500.

Governors

The involvement of governors varied from school to school, as has been described in the decision-making chapter. It is interesting to note, however, the skills and expertise which governors brought with them and the material benefits to the school from links with local business through governor employees.

School 8, situated in a suburban location, was fortunate in the support it received from its governors. The head teacher recognised the skills and expertise which the parent and co-opted governors had brought to the local management of the school. Moreover, these governors often were able to contribute goods or financial support for minor projects on behalf of the companies where they were employed. Local town charities were also very supportive and had contributed £91,000 towards the remodelling and equipping of a new technology block.

A director of a local company on the governing body of School 1 had supported the school substantially with financial support, materials and expertise to assist the School's Environment Committee (made up of staff and pupils) to develop a courtyard garden in the school grounds which had subsequently won a major national competition. Not only had this project enhanced the school environment but it had been a significant motivating factor for pupils. Such support was particularly welcomed by the school.

In School 6 an enthusiastic co-opted industrial governor, who was also Vice Chair of Governors and the Chair of the Finance Committee, had made initial introductions between the school and his company which had resulted in a remodelled technology room, supported financially and with expertise from the company and teacher placement for a period with the company.

Increased community use of school premises

Some schools were increasingly hiring out school premises for the financial benefit of the school, sometimes as part of a long-standing arrangement with the LEA for the provision of community adult education.

School 4 is probably exceptional in its buildings assets. A manor house on the school site, and the original school building, provides an attractive venue for general community use. Lettings of the house have been nearly doubled in the past year from £43,000 to £80,000 and a new appointment of lettings officer is funded from this revenue. The school recognises the potential for external income generated by increased lettings and the new appointment underlines this. The school is also fortunate in benefiting from a Governors' Foundation Fund which has generated large sums of money in recent years through the sale of land in the vicinity. By contrast, in a more modest way, School 1 was also generating extra funds for the school through hiring out school premises and had created a management group to oversee this. However, the school was aware of the value of the support of the local community and the emphasis was on providing the school buildings as a facility for local community use.

Local management is providing the opportunity for schools to develop the use of their facilities in more innovative ways. School 5 was developing a music suite with the intention of organising a self-financing music club for pupils and the local community. As the LEA music service provision had always been held on the other side of the town and, while open to all local pupils, was perceived to 'belong' to pupils attending other schools, this initiative was felt to be an attempt to redress the balance of provision by making use of the school's premises and expertise.

Other schools also recognised that the enhancement of sports facilities would be beneficial to local people who use the facility and also possibly increase the use, thus bringing more revenue to the school. School 3 had used £40,000 from the school budget to enhance the specification of a newly provided Activity Hall (part of an LEA capital project). Improvement of the school's sports facilities and enhancement of the PE curriculum was recognised to have the possible spin-off of increased lettings of the facility to the public. Similarly the swimming pool and changing rooms had been improved not only to enhance facilities for school pupils but also to encourage increased lettings within the community: 'As a consequence of local management we are more conscious of looking outwards to gain financially' (Head).

Adult education

Provision for adult education in the community continued to be a priority for locally managed schools. School 6 had a dual-use arrangement with the Local Education Authority whereby school premises were used for adult education classes out of school hours and a leisure centre on site was a shared facility. While some marginal financial benefit had accrued to the school as a result of this arrangement, it was recognised that the status of the school within its community was important and increasingly so in the context of local management.

The arrangement between School 12 and its LEA on community education presented an interesting case in the context of local management owing to the authority having delegated its budget for continuing education to the school. Thus the school exercised increased control over the delivery of continuing education and made use of increased resources to provide extra facilities for its students as well as community users. School 10, as described above, had collaborated with the local library service to create a community library in an old kitchen, which would be staffed outside school hours at evenings and weekends – an improved facility for the benefit of the school and the community it serves.

School 16 also had a long-standing arrangement with the LEA for use of the premises for an adult education programme. Now, as a grant maintained school, the governing body had made a positive decision to maintain and if possible extend the facility and was in the process of negotiating with the authority: 'We have a responsibility to the local community – much wider than just 9.00–3.00 p.m. It makes the school a richer place if we do this. If we can make a profit this helps to resource the school' (parent governor). The school had a swimming pool which has always been used by the community and grant maintained status was not going to alter this: 'There is no mood to change' (parent governor).

External contractors

It is a consequence of local management that delegated budgets and school-based decision making allow schools to have a free choice over the provision of services. Local management has freed schools from their former ties with local authority contractors, although many of them still retain local authority provided services, particularly for advisory services. The most common areas of change would appear to be cleaning, catering, grounds maintenance, caretaking and minor repairs. However, the majority of these services are being provided in-house. This is covered in more detail in the staffing chapter.

We found little evidence, however, of schools using external contractors. School 3 had set up a limited company, with free professional advice from a parent, to provide cleaning and catering services for the school. It was felt that cleaning was carried out to a much higher standard under the new arrangements for no extra cost, thus releasing funds from the school budget to be used for teaching and learning. Improved provision of school meals and snacks, tailored to the school's needs, was felt to be offering a better and much needed service for pupils, particularly during the lunch-break.

Grant maintained schools requiring assistance on financial and legal matters were buying the services of local solicitors and accountants. As a result the head teacher in School 9 felt they were 'More effective, efficient and business-like.' Another grant maintained school, School 17, was using an ex-LEA adviser on a consultancy basis. The appointment was for two days' teaching commitment and three days' consultancy on learning differentiation.

Industry and commerce

Financial support from local businesses

Many of the information technology initiatives in schools have only been possible through tapping into external support from local industry and commerce. School 6 provides a typical illustration of the entrepreneurial spirit demonstrated in several schools.

School 6 was used by a computer manufacturer as a regional information centre for its equipment in return for which the school received in the region of £22,000 worth of hardware and software in a technology suite. The school also had developed close links with a local manufacturing company. One of the school governors was an employee. A teacher had been placed in the company for training and the company had donated £1,000 towards the refitting of a design technology room. As a result of this the head teacher described the design technology department as rejuvenated. All classes in the school made use of the new facility and the delivery of computer graphics in the curriculum had greatly improved. The head teacher clearly felt he had achieved an important objective: 'the bottom line is to motivate staff'. Also in School 6 another local company had donated £4,000, which was matched with £1,500 from school budget, to develop a professional standard drama studio as part of a new performing arts suite. As a result of this development the head of performing arts felt that the school was becoming well known for its drama capability and had attracted professional theatre companies to come and perform, 'the quality of drama will improve – motivation and attitude has already improved'. More typically, schools recognised the increased difficulty in attracting external funding from industry and commerce in times of recession and it is possible that such commercial deals as described above are by far the exception rather than the rule; much also depends on the location of a school.

Student–industry links

Collaboration with local business for world of work experience was, however, significantly emphasised by schools as part of non-financial external support. School 8 had many external links with local business on curriculum projects, a community fortnight for Year 11 pupils, liaison with local theatre and dance companies and career days.

School 5 had developed strong links with the local business community, through industry days, collaborative work and small financial contributions: 'We network with external sources – there is a mutuality – more human resources than financial' (Head). School 17 has links with 200 local companies for work experience and involved sixth formers in local projects such as Challenge to Industry and Understanding Industry. In addition to this the scheme has created links with local businesses through collaboration on the Young Enterprise Scheme. Industrial governors were also helping to maintain links with local business and bringing benefits to students through work experience, curriculum collaboration and job prospects. These links were described as being based on mutual interest.

Collaboration on staff training

Schools have links with major concerns in their locality whereby the companies provided industrial experience and management training for teaching staff at no charge to the school. Staff who had been involved in management training felt that 'this is improving my effectiveness and therefore hopefully the effectiveness of my teaching and learning for pupils'. School 3 had developed links with the local division of a multi-national company resulting in an annual three-day Industrial Awareness Conference for Year 9 pupils. This was felt to have become an important part of the curriculum and described by the deputy head as 'highly motivating for even the most "turned-off" pupils and an integral part of their experience of industrial awareness'. This school had also used the facilities of a local company for staff training in total quality management. This had involved staff in quality improvement projects and had resulted in more effective and efficient meetings and a more consultative approach to work.

A total quality management project was developed by School 7 in collaboration with a major computer company. This was a pilot project to test a commercial model in a public service environment and involved the school in forming quality groups to consider various issues, such as customer satisfaction. This process would then raise issues which needed to be tackled in the School Development Plan. The head teacher hoped that 'Raising standards of quality will have benefits in the curriculum.'

Training providers

In addition to collaborative links with commercial organisations, schools are buying in the services of other training providers, such as University Schools of Education, for staff development and curriculum project work. The recently formed Training and Enterprise Councils are also a welcome source of external funding for certain training projects.

University sponsored projects and training

School 14 had reorganised the structure of the maths department regarding assessment schemes as a result of being involved in the Southampton University School Maths Project. 'There has been a "drastic" change in the way maths is delivered – it is unlikely that I would have known anything about this area' admitted the maths teacher leading the project.

School 6 had worked with the Centre for the Study of Comprehensive Schools (CSCS) at Leicester University and the National Council for Education Technology at Warwick on curriculum projects. Both had involved use of computers across the curriculum and brought Year 9 pupils in contact with local feeder primary schools. A computer company had loaned hardware and provided expertise and software for the duration of the Leicester project. This was judged by staff to have been an 'outstanding success' and had an impact on teaching staff because it had introduced a student centred approach to learning as Year 9 pupils acted as teachers for younger children.

Training and Enterprise Councils (TECs)

School 9 was involved in a staff training scheme 'Investors in People' provided and part funded by the local TEC. As a local facilitator for training the TECs have provided external funding (usually a system of matched funding) for various school-based projects based on individual school bids. School 8, for example, was awarded funding towards the refurbishment of a careers' library plus funds for staff to develop a new BTec Business and Finance course. School 7 used TEC funding for staff training on the General National Vocational Qualifications (GNVQs) and School 14 was successful in receiving £2,500 TEC funding to develop curriculum links between maths and science. The money was used for equipment and to free staff in order to develop curriculum schemes.

Central government

Reference has already been made in preceding chapters to the use to which schools have put external funding received from central government initiatives. Many of these were making use of TVI funds, a scheme originated prior to local management. More recently central government support for technology has been provided under the Technology Schools Initiative (TSI). School 8 had recently been successful in being awarded £200,000 under this scheme to purchase computer aided design equipment for a new control technology block. This sum was being used together with other external sources of funding to reorganise and revitalise this area of the school's curriculum. School 9 had also been awarded £250,000 in 1992 to modify and extend the accessibility of information technology throughout the curriculum. Accordingly much equipment had been purchased, a technology block had been modified and a modern languages computer suite had been created for whole school use. School 9 had also drawn upon other sources of funding, in this case a Governors' Foundation Fund, to complete the project.

Those schools in the study which had become grant maintained had a further opportunity to bid for government funds reserved specifically for those schools. School 17 had been awarded the biggest amount for a capital building project for a grant maintained school in 1993 getting £700,000 to build a new science block. School 9 has used £75,000 of grant maintained funding to create new office accommodation and general refurbishment of other areas. School 13 had been awarded funding as a grant maintained school to build a new technology block. This had enabled the school to direct existing funding towards a rolling programme of refurbishment of science laboratories which would otherwise not have been possible.

Local government support

Dual-use arrangements

The LEA provided support for schools in many ways. Two schools in the study had dual-use arrangements for part of the site. As a result of this, School 6 had received funding from the local authority to match that provided by the school to remodel the arts faculty. The improved facility would be used by the local authority for adult education classes outside school hours.

Community education funding

School 12 has a closer partnership with its LEA owing to delegation of the community education budget. Access to and planning of the provision for continuing education for the community was mutually agreed between the school and the LEA. This was resulting in many extras being provided for the school, for the benefit of students, which could also be enjoyed by the wider community.

Capital projects

Capital projects funded by the LEA had been recently completed or were nearing completion in six of the schools in the study. These were all large-scale projects either to expand the present school accommodation in response to rising rolls over several years or to rationalise split-site schools onto one site. Clearly these schools found themselves in a very advantageous situation when it came to prioritising and targeting use of their existing resources.

Local Education Authority services

Under local management thus far, local authorities predominantly have centrally funded advisory curriculum services to local schools. Several schools in the study had taken advantage of this service. However, as some local authorities begin to delegate this part of the budget, future arrangements for buying back local authority advisory services or purchasing the services of other external agencies remain unclear.

School 14 also continued to use LEA advisory support particularly on National Curriculum assessment. The school does not have an RE specialist and the support of the RE adviser was particularly welcome. The school had used the LEA Assessment and Recording Achievement Unit to guide and support work on assessment and the accreditation of Records of Achievement. This was felt to be excellent staff development and had a considerable effect on the effectiveness of assessment throughout the school. The deputy head commented: 'This has resulted in our focusing hard on our assessment procedures – the catalyst for the whole process being the LEA.'

School 5 had been involved in LEA co-ordinated projects on two curriculum areas. 'Raising Achievement in Maths' had involved the school in trialling and evaluating good curriculum practice. It was felt that such involvement motivated staff to think in different ways about methods of teaching and helped staff development. The performing arts department of School 6 had participated in an LEA Community Education Initiative for the past three years funded by the LEA up to £1,500 p.a. This involved Years 7 and 8 in theatre workshops and Year 11 pupils taking a production 'on tour' to local feeder primary schools. The effectiveness of the experience is best described by one pupil as 'The most worthwhile educational experience I've ever received in my life.'

Local authority advisory services were used for National Curriculum support through in-service staff training. School 9, which had become grant maintained, still bought into its local authority advisory service whom they found helpful with specific curriculum problems and National Curriculum advice. School 3 also used the LEA advisory service for National Curriculum support and was intending to buy back into the service under an extended delegation package from April 1993.

Thus we may observe that schools' relationships with their local community and their LEA are changing as a result of delegated management of resources. It may be the case that increased school autonomy will have a positive effect on the way in which each community supports its school to enhanced mutual benefit in the future.

IMPROVING COST-EFFECTIVENESS

At the end of the previous chapter we identified a set of characteristics which schools might be expected to have if they sought to be more cost-effective in their use of resources. We recognised that these attributes of cost-effectiveness would be additional to those that might be expected in an effective school. In this final section, our intention is to consider the extent to which these 15 schools have those attributes we suggest would be associated with being a cost-effective school. While it is a theme to which we will return in the closing chapter, a brief consideration of these findings is appropriate.

Our summary of the cost-effective school stressed the importance of a *radical audit* in which resources would be matched to needs on the principle of fitness-for-purpose. We anticipated that the use of premises would be characterised by creativity and diversity and that decisions are being made which differ from those made in the past. The evidence we report suggests that these LM and GM schools are actively engaged on policies which match these characteristics. Schools show changes in senior management to take account of new responsibilities and a readiness to restructure support staff in order to improve administrative and curriculum support. Some of these decisions were creative responses to opportunities that presented themselves and we were not aware of an audit of the overall pattern of work in these schools which, for example, might lead to a systematic review of those parts of a teacher's work that might be done by others. Whether schools can – or should – engage in such a review is a theme we will consider in our closing chapter.

There are schools where information on *costs* is being improved as an aid to decision making and there were many comments on the improvement in financial information. There was, however, little evidence of diversity and creativity in the use of the new financial information systems. We do, however, cite positive comments on the opportunity to plan spending, particularly on premises, over a period of years. Perhaps the most striking example of such forward planning is the curriculum planning of School 10. This was the case where funds of up to £300,000 were being set aside in order to finance a stable sixth form programme during a period of years when a group of small student cohorts would be in the sixth form. It represents a good example of a school using its information on pupil numbers and expected budgets to inform its policy choices – which is not to say that others might have made a different judgement on policy!

The extent of *internal delegation* to departments was apparent from the interviews with heads of department, some being able to make decisions on marginal changes in staffing as well as in the purchase of learning materials. We do also show the boundaries of internal delegation. Decisions on the complement of staff, replacements and dismissals are, typically, the domain of the head teacher and SMT and this has been used to match staff to curriculum requirements in ways that are seen to be a significant improvement on the past. This internal delegation was accompanied by a *dialogue of accountability* within departments and some heads of department cited the departmental plan and its place within the wider School Development Plan. Accounts from the schools also showed the restructuring of decision making as a result of these changes and the greater prominence given to governors. Typically, governors refer to one set of committees and teachers another, only the head teacher and senior staff referring to both. In this respect, School 4 is distinctive: its key Financial and Management Committee is a committee of the governing body but includes elected staff representatives and is referred to by all groups as a major locus of decision.

How the dangers associated with the structural *detachment of management* are addressed is not easily determined from our brief visits. Some accounts from senior managers of the effects on pupils of resource decisions suggest an awareness of their impact. There is also evidence of team meetings where views are exchanged and opinions tested on the needs of the school, and School 8 used a staff questionnaire as part of the audit stage of the Development Plan. These are means whereby the views of teachers on the resources needed to improve the standard and quality of learning can be collected. Whether these are sufficient for management to be adequately informed about the quality of teaching and learning is unclear and, unlike the case study schools, we had no adequate means of further evaluation of these processes. In the case study schools, more extensive interviews and survey data from parents and pupils add to our understanding of this crucial area.

Governors in School 12 undertook a careful review of the annual set of examination results as part of their assessment of the school's performance. This was an unusual example of the use of information that was *independent* of the teachers and head teacher who appear to remain, outside formal inspections, the source of most information on the day-to-day progress of these schools. Whether this is a significant issue for improving cost-effectiveness is a question to which we will return, with others, when we also have evidence from the three case study schools.

CONCLUSION

Our visits to these 15 secondary schools show the great diversity of ways in which use has been made of the powers delegated to schools as a result of LMS and GMS. They provided a basis for more detailed enquiry in three schools. Each of these schools, which we have named Broome, Skelton and Whittaker, were part of the original 18 schools we visited. Owing to our subsequent and extensive visits to these schools, the data collected provide a much richer account of how delegation is being used and with what effect on the quality of teaching and learning.

Chapter 5

Broome School

Encouraging growth

A VIEW OF THE SCHOOL

Broome School is an 11–16 co-educational comprehensive school situated in the central area of a large city. The number on roll is a little over 600 pupils and the standard number is 210. The number on roll has declined slightly since 1987 but the intake trend is now upwards. In 1992 the school admitted 58 per cent of its standard number with 54 per cent having expressed the school as a first choice. The school has an attendance rate which has remained at about 83 per cent since 1987 but is now showing an improvement with 86 per cent in attendance in 1992. The school had no exclusions in 1991–2.

The pupil intake has changed over recent years. Having taken 75 per cent Asian pupils, the school now takes 50 per cent Bengali and Bangladeshi with 5–10 per cent mixed race; 15 per cent of the intake is Afro-Caribbean – a growing sector – and 15 per cent white pupils. In 1992 approximately 70 per cent of the intake have English as a second language and 88 per cent are entitled to free school meals. The school recruits pupils from a wide area within the inner city; 0.3 per cent are statemented for special needs.

In 1993 the school had a teaching staff complement of 37 plus four Section 11 teachers and two teachers of English as a second language. The pupil teacher ratio is 16:1 and the overall average teaching load is 73 per cent. Nine support staff include two full-time technicians, two part-time library assistants, one part-time home economics technician, one part-time reprographics technician, one full-time clerical and two part-time clerical assistants. The school has no vacancies on the governing body which meets twice per term.

The school has been locally managed since April 1990. Owing to the proximity of a number of schools, the pattern of local housing and demographic change in the local area, the school is in a highly competitive situation. The head teacher recognises that maintaining an intake of 600, while a nearby school has only 280, has been an achievement which she attributes to 'vigorous involvement and making sure that the school is known as a deliverer on various major initiatives'. It is because of such initiatives that the school is earning money and remaining solvent. Broome School is a member of the 'Maston Consortium', a partnership between business and education in the inner-city area. As a result it has access to resources under a government scheme to create opportunities in inner-city areas. Since the appointment of a new head teacher the school has developed these and other links with local business and further education colleges. This has resulted in extra funding for office technology, predominantly from the secondment of a senior member of staff to local industry for one year, and the development of vocational and business technology courses in school for women returnees and post-16 students. The development of GNVQ courses for post-16 students in September 1993 is an example of this. Since local management, the head teacher asserts, 'the school looks better, it's got more equipment and more staff'.

The school's formula budget for 1992–3 was about £1.2m. With additions for dual use of the site, amounting to about £10,000, and £25,000 in support from industry for secondment of the senior teacher, the gross budget amounts to £1.25m.

The school works hard at its relationships with the local community and the families of pupils. This aspect of school life was recently commended by HMI: 'The school has well-established and positive community links. It uses these to advantage within the curriculum, particularly in prevocational work, work experience and careers education and guidance'. Leisure facilities have recently been provided, by creating a fully equipped gym/fitness centre, for use by local people as well as pupils. The school also has a parents' room and plans to extend this to include crèche facilities in the near future. The importance of working together with parents to enhance pupils' learning is clearly recognised.

The school is popular with pupils and parents. A survey of Year 9 pupils (Table 5.1) undertaken as part of the project, and which had a response rate of 82 per cent showed high levels of satisfaction, 77 per cent of pupils agreeing with the statement 'I like coming to school'. The response rate from parents (Table 5.2) was lower at 47 per cent and in reply to the statement 'My child likes coming to school', 100 per cent registered agreement.

Table 5.1 Year 9 pupils: Broome School

What I think	strongly agree (%)	agree (%)	disagree (%)	strongly disagree (%)
I like coming to school	14.6	62.5	15.6	7.3
I am unhappy at school	5.2	18.8	55.2	20.8

Table 5.2 Year 9 Parents: Broome School

What I think	strongly agree (%)	agree (%)	disagree (%)	strongly disagree (%)
My child likes coming to school	32.1	67.9	0	0
Most families support this school	21.8	65.5	10.9	1.8
My child is unhappy at school	5.5	7.3	56.4	30.9

A total of 18 examination subjects are offered at GCSE. The trend in examination results between 1990 and 1992 has shown significant improvement in English, art and design and information technology. More generally, the number of Year 11 pupils achieving five or more GCSEs at grades A–C declined from 5.3 per cent in 1989 to 4.6 per cent in 1992. At the end of the academic year 1990–1 just over one-third of Year 11 pupils continued in full-time education whereas nearly one-quarter were placed on training schemes. The examination results for 1994, however, show a sharp improvement: 13 per cent of Year 11 pupils achieved five or more GCSEs at grades A–C, compared with 4.6 per cent in 1992, and 56 per cent obtained five or more A–G grades, compared with 15.5 per cent in 1992.

The recent HMI report on the school acknowledged that it has 'many satisfactory and some good features, but also some major weaknesses in the standards achieved by pupils'. It recognised that 'Results in GCSE examinations are improving gradually from a very low base'. In particular the school's efforts 'to improve the standards of and attitudes to reading with lower school pupils' is noted.

The report comments upon the quality of the learning environment, pupil behaviour, the good relationships and mutual respect shown between pupils and staff, and amongst pupils, together with the positive efforts being made by teachers to 'provide an education which is appropriate for all the pupils'. Perhaps most significantly, senior management is recognised for 'developing appropriate strategies to improve the quality of the school, and using its budget effectively to do so'. These indicators of school improvement will be referred to, in the light of analysis of the research data, in subsequent sections.

RESOURCE USE AND OUTCOMES

School budget share is very tight – we use as much as possible for staffing – around 85% which is high. School budget share is the only guaranteed revenue so as Head I need to investigate other sources of capital to take pressure off. I have set aside more time recently to publicise a positive profile of the school so that bids for money are more credible.

(head teacher)

Broome School has concentrated its focus for resource allocation on its learning environment. Raising the standards of the school environment, through improvements to school buildings and site, was identified as a contributory step towards school improvement. Thus, the school grounds are being improved, existing school buildings adapted for more specific use and, with improved equipment and materials, facilities for delivery of the curriculum enhanced. Funding has been raised from a variety of sources, both school budget and external grants. The inner-city location provides the opportunity for the school to bid for external funding allocated to the region.

The school library

The emphasis on the development of the school library was sponsored by the head teacher, and the opportunity of the appointment of a new head of English was taken to include overall responsibility for the library within the job description. An 'A' allowance was also given to one post-holder within the English department for special responsibility for the library. A project approach to revitalising library provision was adopted. As well as enhanced staffing, the existing accommodation was decorated and new furniture provided. £7,000 was made available for books and video equipment. In order to provide funding for continuing resource provision, 10 per cent of each department's capitation budget was allocated to library resources. A training day on the new provision was set aside for all staff.

The improved facility was clearly having an impact on the whole school. Staff at all levels acknowledged the improvement: 'The environment in the library is warm and caring, children need this sort of environment to help them enjoy what they are doing, e.g. learning to read, watching videos.' Another member of teaching staff commented: 'The library is a very pleasant and positive working area – used by pupils a lot.' The library was used for approximately ten periods per week by staff for teaching pre-vocational courses, geography, religious education, English and science. At other times smaller groups of pupils might use the area. The video facility was booked as appropriate. Only one member of the teaching staff had expressed frustration due to the lack of a booking procedure for whole class teaching – an issue which had since been addressed. The same teacher expressed some disquiet over how much staff and pupils were, in practice, making use of the new facilities.

It was certainly the case, however, that the provision of more support staff made the library more accessible to pupils. The new materials and equipment were seen as facilitating work on pupil projects and their information retrieval skills. This also presents pupils with the opportunity to develop an understanding of the library cataloguing system: 'it has given pupils the incentive to research and do project based work'. The emphasis on providing facilities for pupils to develop research skills was made together with the opportunity to help improve reading skills: 'The library has helped in improving the reading in school which was identified as a priority.'

Teaching staff also recognised the improved resources available to the whole school and welcomed the pooling of departmental funds to provide books:

The library has helped enormously with the shortage of text books – we all chip in and can decide on which books we buy.

The library has certainly improved resources for the whole school – needed to be a priority – modernised a previously out of date resource for the benefit of all Departments.

Recently I have been doing a 'Holiday' topic with Year 9 – the main aim is research and I'm working with the librarian to create information packs.

Pupils appear to appreciate the development. Table 5.3 shows that in the survey of Year 9 pupils, 71 per cent agreed that the library is excellent. Some pupils act as librarians and there is a library club and a homework club. Parents had also noticed the impact and Table 5.4 shows that, when presented with the same question, 88 per cent of Year 9 parents also agreed. Pupil use of the library, however, may need further encouragement: 36 per cent said they used the library at lunch time more than they used to and 39 per cent said they used the library in lesson time more than they used to.

The impact of new developments may take time. The head of English summed up the project as a whole school learning issue 'enhancing the learning environment'.

New computer network and refurbishment of technology suites

Improved facilities in the school for information technology were funded through external sources. Funds generated from the secondment of a senior teacher were matched by school budget share and the local TEC which, in turn, acted as a lever in bidding for funding from other sources for a second phase of technology resourcing.

To facilitate improved access to information technology across the curriculum the computer network is being upgraded. Clusters of computers are now in the majority of departments and more easily accessible in teaching rooms. There are computer suites for business studies and graphics; computers in each maths classroom, a computer cluster in the English department and in the humanities department. All staff are being

Table 5.3 Year 9 pupils: Broome School

What I think	strongly agree (%)	agree (%)	disagree (%)	strongly disagree (%)
I like coming to school	14.6	62.5	15.6	7.3
I use the library at lunch time more than I used to	7.3	29.2	43.8	19.6
A well-decorated classroom makes me want to work harder	15.5	45.4	28.9	10.3
Often there are not enough books to go round	37.5	42.7	14.6	5.2
The inside of the school is better decorated than when I first came	21.9	59.4	12.5	6.3
I hardly ever get to use computers at school	21.6	30.9	36.1	11.3
I find school work interesting	10.9	57.6	25.0	6.5
The outside areas around the school have been improved since I started at the school	48.4	38.9	5.3	7.4
We get to use more new books than when I first came	22.7	48.5	20.6	8.2
The school needs decorating	28.9	39.2	23.7	8.2
The school is cleaner and tidier than it used to be	10.5	47.4	32.6	9.5
The corridors and classrooms look nicer than when I first came	17.0	48.9	30.9	3.2
I use computers in my work more often than when I first came	25.0	30.2	27.1	17.7
I use the library in lesson time more than I used to	8.2	30.9	35.1	25.8
The school is well off for books and equipment	6.5	35.9	42.4	15.2
The school's library is excellent	24.5	46.8	20.2	8.5

inducted through in-house training from staff within the technology department.

The upgraded system is welcomed by staff, particularly as the existing network was unreliable. Pupils appeared to be making use of the improved facilities and 55 per cent of Year 9 pupils surveyed felt that they used computers now more than in the past. Parents also showed a more positive response, 64 per cent disagreeing with the statement 'My child hardly ever gets to use computers at school'. The network and the response to it may reflect a gap between what is feasible in terms of provision and expectations. Staff were pleased with the development of their computer capacity but it may remain well short of parent and pupil expectations.

Several staff commented on the improved facilities. The computer suite, in particular, was seen as a means for improving the presentation of the work of pupils in business studies and graphics. The head of technology felt that the new desk top publishing area was being widely used by both staff and pupils and 'has improved the presentation of work generally and broadened horizons'. He explained the pressing need for more computers in all areas in response to National Curriculum requirements for information technology, although some time ago one computer was provided for each department. Refurbishment of the computer suite in the business studies department had ensured better facilities for desk-top publishing and graphics and a further suite would be completed later in the year to offer post-16 facilities to study GNVQs. Consequently, it was too early to judge the impact of such new course provision.

Landscaping and general refurbishment

Internal and external refurbishment of the school premises and grounds had recently begun as part of a rolling programme. External funding from the Department of the Environment and the LEA has provided £200,000 for the improvement of the school site and its sports facilities. A rolling programme of internal decoration and refurbishment is in place under the supervision of a senior teacher with responsibility for resources co-ordination. As part of this programme new display boards, new furniture and new carpets have been purchased. About 25 per cent of the school is now carpeted, all classrooms and corridors have been repainted and eight to ten classrooms have new furniture. Senior management stressed that the development of the programme would be determined by departments identifying their own needs and that staff would have a say in what was carried out.

Funding for the improvement of grounds was enabling landscaping of the site including the creation of a quadrangle area with seating. The sports pitch will also be resurfaced.

Staff readily acknowledged the importance of environment as a motivating factor. The school site had become run down and in need of attention. Now it was described as 'a more attractive place of learning' and 'important for the well being of everyone'. Other staff expressed disquiet on the use of funds for such purposes when they could still identify needs for curriculum resources. However, as these funds could only be used for urban development the school was bound by external factors as to how the financial aid could be utilised.

The impact of premises and grounds improvement would appear to have been more significant for pupils and parents. Our survey (Tables 5.3 and 5.4) showed 87 per cent of pupils and 98 per cent of parents agreeing with the statement that 'The outside areas around the school have

Table 5.4 Year 9 parents: Broome School

What I think	strongly agree (%)	agree (%)	disagree (%)	strongly disagree (%)
The school is in a poor state of repair	5.6	22.2	50.0	22.2
Often there are not enough books to go round	11.3	45.3	35.8	7.5
My child hardly ever gets to use computers at school	13.5	25.0	38.5	23.1
The outside areas around the school have been improved since my child started at the school	29.6	68.5	1.9	0
There aren't enough computers at the school	9.6	34.6	36.5	19.2
The school needs decorating	11.3	39.6	35.8	13.2
The school is cleaner and tidier than it used to be	14.5	69.1	12.7	3.6
Rooms and corridors are better decorated than they used to be	22.6	64.2	13.2	0
The school buys a lot of new books	17.6	47.1	29.4	5.9
The school often looks dirty	0	11.8	56.9	31.4
The school is well off for books and equipment	14.0	46.0	38.0	2.0
The school's library is excellent	25.5	62.7	7.8	3.9

improved'. To statements on the decoration of the school, 81 per cent of pupils agreed that the school is better decorated although 50 per cent of parents believed the school needs decorating with 84 per cent agreeing that the school is cleaner and tidier. These replies and other comments showed much pupil and parent support for the enhanced environment and that redecoration, carpeting of classrooms and a tidier and cleaner environment had not gone unnoticed.

Our interview and survey data show that the projects outlined above have all been welcomed by staff, and acknowledged as desirable not only for pupils but also for the local community. The effect on teaching and learning was recognised as being a long-term strategy as the school gradually becomes better able to deliver an entitlement curriculum for all pupils. There was a sense of regeneration and remotivation. Despite certain members of staff and some pupils having difficulty in reconciling short-term priorities with the longer-term view, much satisfaction was expressed for the future:

Having been in the school for many years I feel that the resources and general fabric of the building are now better than of the past. I feel the finances are being carefully looked after and staff generally are becoming more aware about their own role in being responsible for their own budgets.

Certain small-scale alterations to premises had been possible under local management. A classroom has been converted into a meeting room for parents where refreshments could be served and there were plans further to develop the area with crèche facilities. This provides a tangible expression of the value which the school places on links with the families of pupils and the rhetoric of welcome becomes a reality. Two classrooms have been converted into one larger area, creating a base for specialist language teachers who give support to new pupils arriving in the area from abroad. In such a way the learning environment is enhanced and the importance of this part of the school's work is highlighted.

Additional curriculum materials have also been funded. Some departments have bid successfully for equipment and books, in excess of the basic capitation budget. The science department has had £250 to purchase new text books. The English department has purchased videos of Shakespeare plays for use in class and had funds for new books and a tape recorder for use in Key Stage 3. Other staff mentioned the provision of new blinds, furniture, display boards, new blackboards and notice boards, an overhead projector and screen and filing cabinets. In the home economics department hand basins had been installed in all kitchen areas. The issue of curriculum resources is still emphasised by some members of staff for future funding: 'I believe that more money should be available for day to day needs – paper, pens, pencils, other equipment'. Another commented, 'I also like text books and class readers that don't fall apart.' One of the potential difficulties with delegated management of resources may, however, be raised expectations. Within cash limited budgets, priority decisions have to be made and not all needs can be met immediately.

The perceptions of pupils and parents on books and equipment reinforce this view: 81 per cent of pupils feel that often there are not enough books to go round and only 42 per cent feel that the school is well off for books and equipment. While 56 per cent of parents feel that there are not enough books to go round, 65 per cent acknowledge that the school does buy a lot of new books.

Additional teaching staff

Resources have not been targeted solely at physical resources. Extra funding has also been used to provide additional staffing. Funds sufficient to meet the costs of two extra teaching staff have been transferred from the traditional supply cover budget. This was made possible as a result of an agreement with teaching staff to share supply cover between themselves, in return for covering the classes of absent colleagues. On average this gives less than half an hour per week of non-contact time additional to the existing 4–5 hours per week. The school budget has also been used to pay ancillary staff in response to specific needs. For example, one member of staff is paid for five hours per week to support one pupil with particular difficulties.

The impact of extra teaching staff is considerable. Smaller pupil groups more easily facilitate different kinds of teaching groups, for example setting/whole year/mixed ability and time for Records of Achievement work. There are no longer any unqualified staff teaching groups in maths or science.

RESOURCE MANAGEMENT

Since the appointment of a new head teacher, five years ago, the school has developed new structures for decision making in the context of local management. The creation of these structures and the development planning process – discussed more fully in the following section – has been initiated by the head teacher, supported by the Senior Management Team.

The structures of decision making

The school's governing body meets twice each term and operates a committee structure with responsibility for executive decision making. Four committees exist for school development planning, personnel, finance and premises. The committees each meet once prior to each full Governing Body Meeting, a total of eight meetings per term. The head teacher plus four governors sit on each committee, each of which has its own terms of reference reviewed at the beginning of each academic year. Three standing committees exist: a first committee and an appeals committee to deal with staff grievances, and an exclusions committee.

The Senior Management Team of seven meets weekly. Its main function is to discuss policy and to share information on school developments. It comprises the head teacher, three deputy head teachers, two heads of school who co-ordinate Key Stage 3 and Key Stage 4 respectively and a senior teacher with responsibility for the co-ordination of resources. A redefinition of the senior management functions within the school has taken place in recent years. Two heads of school posts have been developing with increased responsibility for the co-ordination of National Curriculum Key Stage 3 and Key Stage 4 respectively, an adaptation of posts which had previously been predominantly pastoral in their focus.

The main whole school committee is the Academic Board, comprising heads of faculty and chaired by the curriculum deputy. This group meets at least twice per half term to discuss whole school issues and priorities. It provides a forum for the exchange of ideas between representatives of senior management and representatives from each faculty. In this way all faculties have the opportunity to participate in prioritising and implementing school initiatives. The forum also exists to facilitate the flow of information both to and from departments to senior management. Items for the agenda of this meeting can be tabled by any member of staff.

In addition to the Academic Board there are several smaller School Development Groups, usually comprising no more than six or seven staff with one member of the Senior Management Team. These are cross-faculty groupings and are deliberately not department based. At an annual review, staff have a choice of which group to join. These groups are encouraged to be autonomous and set their own agenda based on current school issues and concerns, with the aim of informing the school development planning process. The purpose of such groups is to give all staff the opportunity to become involved in the whole school development process aside from their individual departmental perspective. The groups meet once every six weeks and minutes are made public. Senior management provides the feedback from the groups to the Senior Management Team.

Academic Areas meet as a team once a month to co-ordinate departmental business, share good practice and to brief and debrief staff on issues from the Academic Board. All minutes from the meetings are circulated within departments and forwarded to the curriculum deputy. Senior management is represented quite broadly across the departments although no formal links exist. There are whole staff meetings once per half term and Monday morning briefings which link with a bulletin issued at the end of each week. If necessary other staff briefings are convened for urgent business. The agendas for the formal meetings are circulated to all staff for items to be included. The value of such a large gathering is questioned by the head teacher who feels that the smaller School Development Groups have taken over as a more meaningful forum for discussion of current issues.

The school makes use of *ad hoc* task groups or open forum meetings, where appropriate. These are briefings which staff may attend voluntarily on issues of current concern and interest. For example, a recent group looked at the National Vocational Qualification. While the school has set up task groups in the past it was acknowledged that this technique might be made more use of in the future.

The Development Plan

The school had no development plans prior to the academic year 1989–90 when the head teacher wrote the first version. As a new management process, development planning had to be introduced gradually and its success necessarily depends on the response of staff, particularly middle management, in shaping that process. The head teacher also wrote the development plan for 1990–91 but with the involvement of more staff. For 1991–2, a cycle was beginning to emerge, partly as a result of senior management's concern with long term plans and priorities for the school. Senior management staff supported each department in putting together its own Development Plan by the end of March/April with projections for the year, including in-service training and its cost. The emphasis at this stage is on all staff participating in the process as fully as possible, in order that senior management may produce a whole school overview in line with long term priorities and goals. From the departmental stage, senior management then distils the school plan into ten priorities, some of which may be carried forward from the previous year.

The two main groupings which inform the school development planning process are the staff School Development Groups, which meet during the year to consider development issues, and the School Development Committee of the governing body which is the forum where governors are involved in the process. The school is unusual in having a committee of that name; the more usual pattern is for schools to have a Curriculum Committee of the governing body (Arnott, Bullock and Thomas, 1992). However, the title necessarily gives the committee a focus and helps underline the importance of development planning within the school. Similarly, the cross-faculty School Development Groups for the staff highlight their involvement in what is an attempt at bringing about a cultural change. These formal structures demonstrate the commitment of senior management to bringing the development planning process to the centre of the school organisation and, thereby, provide opportunities for both staff and governor involvement in the process. In this way, the school's movement towards an effective process of development planning is fostered and supported.

The School Development Plan for 1992–3 sets out whole school priorities with a breakdown of each into targets for the year. The link with use of resources is made through reference to staff members' responsibilities against each target:

Priority: Raising of Pupil Achievement
* The Senior staff will act as mentors to pupils with higher level potential. Parental collaboration and monitoring of course work and assessments will support achievement of higher levels. Staff: Senior Management Team.

Where appropriate, requirements for professional development, equipment and premises modifications are highlighted:

Priority: Classroom Management and Teaching Methodology
* The development of teaching methodologies will be considered through school based INSET provided by the Curriculum Support Service. Twilight sessions offering workshops on Effective Learning will lead to trialling of developments in classes. Staff: Curriculum Deputy.

Priority: Developing Information Technology
* Development of Information Technology across the curriculum with improved resourcing of discrete areas and general classrooms. Desk Top Publishing suite to be established in Technology.

Some targets, however, would have little or no impact on use of resources:

Priority: Punctuality and Attendance
* Rewards for 100% weekly class attendance.

A planning structure has, therefore, begun to shape the development of the school and there are clearly identifiable links between proposed developments and the allocation of resources. This structure operates within organisational processes and these are the subject of the following sections, the first of which focuses on whole school management.

Processes of whole school management

The head teacher has described the school management structure as having been transformed from a school with an 'autonomous Head who made all the decisions ... to it now being a reasonable democratic structure'. She acknowledges that this has required people 'to grow into realising that their opinions are now worth having and that they can change policy'. Having for the past four years depended on her 'out of respect not out of lack of interest' she feels that the school has a governing body that is 'reasonably active'. The Senior Management Team, she asserts, has 'grown remarkably over five years' and now comprises a 'vigorous supportive team', notwithstanding considerable development and change in the role of each of the deputies.

The role of the governing body

While LMS formally allocates responsibility for resource allocation to the governing body, in practice the senior management identifies and implements resource allocations and then accounts for these decisions to the governing body. It may be significant that no member of the teaching staff refers to the governing body as part of the decision-making process. As with the teaching staff, the head teacher has endeavoured to empower the governing body in the decision-making process: 'I don't have to be as tediously long winded as I used to because I've got these committee people (governors) who have actually helped me with the decisions along the way so I can be much briefer.' However, at the governors' meetings we observed, little or no discussion took place on many important resource issues, such as changes to the staff salary structure or School Development Plan projects. In the main, senior management accounted to governors for decisions taken and provided information for future priorities. This may have been accountability by listening but it was not a dialogue. Nonetheless, a governor who is also a local business man contributed to the governors Finance Committee and questioned for example the issue of refuse collection and business rates. In addition, the Chair of governors, a parent, asked very practical questions on the pastoral implications for pupils with the introduction of post-16 courses. Other aspects of this innovation were not queried. Often governor questions, which were not part of senior management's agenda, were set aside.

Governors are being encouraged to work more closely with the school, and the head teacher together with a governor who is also a local authority adviser, was taking the lead. A rolling programme of staff presentations on the curriculum has been initiated for governing body meetings and the departmental development plans form part of the agenda for the governors' School Development Committee. This link was described by the head teacher as providing opportunities only for 'superficial monitoring' by governors. Governors to whom we spoke saw their role in the management process as strategic. The Chair described her role as to 'oversee the general running of the school . . . to ensure that the National Curriculum is delivered to all pupils'. Another acknowledged that he could bring his own professional expertise to bear in management decisions:

> I can reflect the current economic trends onto educational policy and provide information about the requirements of the labour market and current vocational trends. My role is to . . . give specific advice in areas such as corporate buying, health and safety issues, maintenance, budgeting and services.

While the Chair demonstrated much involvement with the school commensurate with governor responsibilities, it was doubtful whether all governors were able to give such commitment to the task.

In this respect, the perceptions of parents with regard to the governing body and their own role in the management of the school is noteworthy (Table 5.5). All parents agreed with the statement that having a governing body is a good thing for the school and 74 per cent would like more of a say in how the school spends its money. However, fewer than 2 per cent of parents in our survey claimed that they knew the name of the Chair of the governing body.

Table 5.5 Year 9 parents: Broome School

What I think	strongly agree (%)	agree (%)	disagree (%)	strongly disagree (%)
Having a governing body is a good thing for the school	47.3	52.7	0	0
I would like more of a say in how the school spends its money	18.0	56.0	24.0	2.0

The role of the head teacher and the Senior Management Team

The role of the head teacher should not be underestimated in moving the school towards an emphasis on development planning. She takes the lead in governing body meetings and its committees and her presence is felt in supporting senior management at the Academic Board. She has a clear vision for the school and is working hard on raising its profile within the local community, in partnership with a range of local agencies. In doing so, she has had to convince staff that the school is not 'fire proof' and that an appreciation of a high profile 'is essential to our existence'. She feels that staff are beginning to understand this and realise that this is 'for the good of Broome School not just for my ego'. She recognises that she leads a lot and initiates many projects, 'but I think that's permeated at least 50% of the staff', and hopes the rest are beginning to feel the benefits of local management. She acknowledges that staff will be stretched and tired but recognises that, in her estimation, they have 'come on leaps and bounds ... confident individuals who are far more ready to do things now than they would have been three or four years ago'.

The recent development of the school library is an example of the head teacher taking an initiative, alongside a newly appointed head of English, who was fully involved in the implementation of the project.

The role of the Senior Management Team is significant in taking decisions on resources, developing a sense of whole school priorities and focusing on long term as well as short term needs. The decision over administrative support systems, for example, purchased for assistance with assessment, was a senior management decision:

It's the job of management to test and filter the system before selling it to staff: it is important to protect staff and introduce new systems at a level they can cope with. It is important for staff to concentrate on teaching and learning.

(deputy head)

The role of senior management appeared to be understood and accepted by the majority of staff, particularly those in middle management roles who had more contact with senior staff on resource issues. The recent decision to attach a member of senior management to a School Development Group was beginning to reinforce their involvement in the school development planning process, as facilitators rather than those who set the agenda. The formal attachment of senior staff to a particular curriculum department is also reinforcing their support role, often in informal as well as formal situations.

Staff participation

How have staff responded to this apparent pressure to undertake increased individual responsibility and become involved in a more open and participatory style of management? Is there a growing sense of ownership of the decision-making process? Certainly, the cycle of formal meetings is providing a structure to ensure development and the School Development Groups and Academic Board appear to work as forums for information and discussion.

The agenda for the Academic Board is put together by the Chair, the curriculum deputy, although any member of staff may table items. The head teacher attends the meetings and, in one which we observed, gave strong support to the Chair in reinforcing policy implementation. We observed some tension between the senior management agenda and the response of faculty heads, although participation was encouraged in the meeting and many did make useful contributions. Questions and comments were invited on all agenda items but often none were made. Both senior management and staff members commented on the importance of this forum for the articulation of the voice of staff, although concern was expressed as to whether 'you were being listened to'.

School Development Groups, although more informal due to the small numbers attending, reinforced the senior management's lead in setting the issues in the meeting: 'others felt able to contribute though didn't have much to say'. A member of senior management acknowledged:

School Development Groups are very important for the involvement of staff. I am quite sure that the Head will make decisions in the final analysis – that's quite right and necessary. I feel as if I have a voice, however, and can influence.

Another member of staff said she understood whole school priorities 'to some extent' and felt that senior staff concerned with particular priorities would relay information to staff as appropriate. However, she was not always aware of the priorities of other departments. The issue of time was recognised by one head of department: 'Some decisions have to be taken quickly by the Head on external funding – I understand this. It is legitimately her role – I have a full timetable.'

A tension between whole school and departmental priorities appears to exist. Certain departments felt that their need for increased funds for everyday materials was pressing and not being met at the expense of the whole school developments. In commenting on recent development projects, one member of staff said: 'I think they're all suitable but I believe that more money should be available for day to day needs – paper, pens, pencils and other equipment.' There may be some misconceptions amongst staff as to how earmarked external funding is being used alongside the school budget. While other departments felt that they were not necessarily getting their fair share of resourcing, despite being in greatest need, senior management was taking a very firm line with departmental heads who were not clearly identifying needs as part of the development planning process. However, there remains some confusion in some quarters as to how departmental budgets are allocated and how much funding is available within the bid system in order to gain extra funding during the year. One member of staff would welcome 'much clearer guidelines as to what money is for', particularly in the light of changing National Curriculum requirements which made it difficult for departments to plan ahead.

Processes of management in faculties and departments

If whole school decisions on resource allocation are to be translated into classroom practice, a feeling of ownership and empowerment at the level of the faculty and department will influence the capacity of staff to carry them through. As has been mentioned, senior management is intent on transforming the school into a culture of development planning which, in order to be effective, depends on the active participation of staff and middle management.

The role of the head of department

Departments were reacting quite differently to the new regime. The role of the head of faculty or head of department appeared to be instrumental in shaping a department's attitude to development planning. Indeed, such middle managers are pivotal figures in translating policy into practice and mediators in assuaging tensions which do appear. As one member of staff put it: 'Senior management do not always have an appreciation of problems experienced by Departments in terms of resources. New developments/ changes in National Curriculum etc. cannot always be written into department plans. Extra funding to cover these changes would be useful.'

The head of an Academic Area is the key link between whole school priorities, as ultimately determined by senior management, and the needs of the departmental team. The significance of the Academic Board, the regular forum for faculty heads and senior management, is consequently underlined as the link with faculty teams.

Staff as part of the departmental team

The science faculty provides an illustration of how departments are translating education resource management into enhanced teaching and learning. The departmental meeting provides an opportunity for the head of department to bring the team up to date on administrative matters. This is common practice from our general observations of departmental meetings. The meetings are held once per half term and all staff attend. In the science faculty, for example, it was noticeable that the laboratory technician played a full part in the proceedings and was encouraged to contribute, particularly on departmental funding for consumables as she was responsible for its day-to-day management: a 'stock take' of consumables was an agenda item at the departmental meeting observed. The head of department was clearly concerned and trying to cut back on consumables to meet a tight budget. Staff were made fully aware of the budget implications and invited to comment on future needs and priorities. Ultimately, however, it was the head of department who summed up the situation and took the responsibility, based on consultation from the meeting, to investigate future spending.

Items from the School Development Plan, raised at the Academic Board, also appeared on the departmental meeting agenda. In particular, the science faculty was later than other departments in identifying GCSE pupils assessed as capable of marked improvement with some additional support. This was a whole school priority to raise standards achieved at GCSE, and senior management was taking time with small groups of pupils with their exam work. Based on recent progress tests, a full discussion took place whereby staff identified suitable candidates for the head of department to forward to senior management. Similarly the INSET arrangements put forward at the Academic Board were briefly discussed pending a decision from senior management, although the head of department seemed confident that the department would get all the training it had requested. The head of department summed up his attitude to the budget responsibilities as:

> democratic at departmental level at meetings – occasionally I will pull rank – we are going to spend £500 on books out of capitation. . . . capitation to departments isn't published but I'm told that science gets more than any others. . . . not sure about the weighting for consumables – I think there is some but I don't know how this is organised . . . a new technician is helping us in organising the department . . . maybe I could give a budget to her – but its early days yet.

Clearly the technician was being involved already, as she pointed out: 'within the science department, discussion takes place on how the year's capitation is to be spent . . . I am actively involved in this and have a reasonable amount of influence with what equipment and chemicals are needed more urgently than others'. The department would appear to be working well as a team. The technician feels:

> I am included in departmental business ... I socialise with staff and I am invited to all departmental meetings even if it doesn't concern me. I am asked about my INSET needs. There's no 'us and them' – the department is very friendly – I'm just one of the staff.

Other departmental meetings we observed also included curriculum organisation on the agenda. Maths looked at a Year 7 activity and discussed programme planning, while also evaluating GCSE results and monitoring assessment tests. English also discussed audit sheets for the curriculum, spelling and a reading assessment for the new intake of pupils. Monitoring and evaluation of teaching and learning is an important part of the process of enhancing quality and forms part of the development planning process. It would seem to be the case that at Broome School some of the departments have travelled further down this road than others. However, such departmental activity will be crucial in identifying how best to improve the teaching and learning process and in turn will inform decisions on how to allocate resources to achieve such ends.

CONCLUSION: ENCOURAGING GROWTH

Broome School illustrates how schools can improve by using the responsibilities of local management as opportunities for development. In creating these opportunities, the head teacher has played a key role and her vision has been the driving force in bringing about new developments. These changes relate both to the core purpose of improving learning and to the way in which management and planning contribute to that core activity. If our earlier analysis of the cost-effective school has any empirical value, we might expect to see some of our proposed characteristics in the changes in management and planning at this school. In this section, therefore, we shall draw upon two 'vignettes' of change at Broome – the development of the library and the computer centre – as part of a more general examination of whether those attributes of the cost-effective school are present in the school.

Development of the school library and the computer suite and network are characterised by some degree of *radical audit*. In both cases, accommodation has been decorated and new furniture purchased; refurbishment of the computer suite in the business studies department drawing upon outside funding negotiated by the head teacher. In the library, additional staffing and responsibility allowances have been allocated and long term funding earmarked from the budgets of departments, this last decision presented as a means of emphasising the place of the library as a resource for use by departments. Setting aside training days, one on the potential of the library and how it might be used and another on the use of IT, conveyed their importance to staff, whose comments recognise the value of these developments. The use of training days is an important recognition that changing the practice of teachers requires preparation.

Our data on these cases do not show how financial *costs* were analysed. In the case of the library, however, the decision to earmark funds from departments was a deliberate move to shape the perceptions of teaching staff about the importance of the library as a learning resource. In this respect, the decision represents a form of opportunity-cost analysis with an explicit recognition of forgone opportunities for departments; our text shows a number of staff were unhappy with the availability of learning materials. The development of the computer suite shows the benefits of the head teacher's ability to draw upon external funding to bring about changes in the premises. It also ensures that the school can provide some post-16 facilities to study for GNVQs.

Responsibility for the day-to-day management of both these initiatives belongs to the respective heads of department and, in this respect, there is clearly *internal delegation*. The strategic decision to pursue these changes, however, was taken at a more senior level. That this should be the case reflects evidence from the schools examined in the previous chapter, where we recognise a differentiation of areas of decision making. It also reflects the firm leadership of the head teacher and her readiness to make decisions and pursue change. The nature and extent of dialogue preceding these decisions is a commentary on the *dialogue of accountability* in the school. Our general account of decision making in the school – which was linked in our interviews to specific developments like the library and computer suite – shows a structure designed to ensure that governors and teachers have opportunities for discussing proposals for change. This structure and the meetings associated with it can serve to reduce the dangers of the *detachment of management* because they act as a source of information *for* management as well as being a means by which management *tells* others what is going to happen. At its present stage of development, the dialogue at Broome is weak. The meetings attended by governors were characterised by much listening on their part, although we note that their participation did include a practical discussion of pastoral implications for proposed changes as well as governors who drew on their particular expertise. Many of the meetings of teachers with senior staff were also characterised by listening on the part of teachers, although we also drew attention to their contribution. These meetings do, none-theless, provide forums where concerns could be transmitted to manage-ment and our interview and survey data suggest that senior management does have the support of teaching and non-teaching staff, parents and pupils for development priorities of which the library and computer suite are examples. For all that, there is a concern about the level of resources for learning materials.

We recognise that the head teacher is aware of the limited nature of the existing dialogue and, while she pushes the school to develop the quality of its education, she also interprets her role as one of encouraging staff and governors to become more active partners. Her earlier comment merits repetition: 'they have come on leaps and bounds . . . confident individuals who are far more ready to do things now than they would have been three or four years ago'. This current state of participation at Broome places a limit on the development and use of sources of information *independent* of head teachers. On the other hand, the head teacher does use information which is independent of teachers, collecting and reviewing the written work of pupils at regular intervals. Together with monitoring the performance of potential high achievers it is a good example of how management is directly focused on learning issues and information.

That the decisions being made may be broadly right is manifest in reactions from within the school community, comments from both staff and governors indicating an optimistic mood:

Positive enhancement since the school has been locally managed. Freedom of decision making both on a financial basis and developmental basis. Creative management and a refreshing approach has created the ethos that exists in the school.

(Broome School: ancillary staff member)

The school is becoming an even more highly focused caring local environment. The Head teacher and staff have shown an even greater ownership of issues and have approached emerging changes as challenges and with courage. The need to understand management techniques is recognised. There is much energy for innovation and improvement and evidence of highly resourceful methodology.

(Broome School: governor)

This positive response is also evident in the wider local community, reactions from parents (Table 5.6) and pupils demonstrating a perception of a well-regarded head teacher and school. The leadership of the head teacher is strongly endorsed: 93 per cent of parents who replied to our survey agreed with the statement 'The school is well led by the head teacher' and 48 per cent expressed strong agreement with the statement. The education offered to pupils is clearly valued, 73 per cent of parents disagreeing with the statement 'What is done at school won't help my child get a job'. The appearance of the school is also appreciated, 88 per cent of parents disagreeing with the statement 'The school often looks dirty'. All this, despite the fact that 60 per cent acknowledge that the school does not seem to have a lot of money.

Table 5.6 Year 9 parents: Broome School

What I think	strongly agree (%)	agree (%)	disagree (%)	strongly disagree (%)
The school is well led by the head teacher	48.1	44.4	3.7	3.7
The school seems to have a lot of money	12.0	28.0	50.0	10.0
The school often looks dirty	0	11.8	56.9	31.4
What is done at school won't help my child get a job	13.2	13.2	47.2	26.4

Set against this are the indications of concern about some decisions. These are not a matter of legitimate concern for the present but a specific challenge for this school and its head teacher is how it manages the move towards the more participatory process envisaged by the head teacher. For the time being, however, there are many more tasks and challenges to be met and overcome at Broome School and the budget will remain a constraint on the achievement of some of its priorities. The optimistic vision of the head teacher is, however, a motivating factor which cannot be ignored. It may be that this is best summed up by one of the Year 9 pupils: 'Broome School is a very good school. It's improving all the time in technology and learning. It may not be the best but to me it is number one!'

Chapter 6

Skelton High School
Initiating and supporting improvement

A VIEW OF THE SCHOOL

Skelton High is a school for 11–16-year-olds situated on the southern edge of a conurbation in the north of England. It draws most of its students – the word used for all the young people at the school – from the relatively prosperous residential areas near which it is situated and there has been a strong expression of parental preference for the school in recent years. In January 1992 the school had 1,195 students on roll and enrolment is on a rising trend.

The school has 69.85 full time equivalent (fte) teachers, 10.3 fte support staff and has been locally managed since April 1991. In 1992–3, its budget share was £2m. In 1993–4 the budget share went up to £2.1m., an increase of 2.8 per cent. Student numbers have increased by 40 students (3.4 per cent) from 1,190 in September 1992 to 1,230 in September 1993. Student performance in public examinations is described by HMI as commendable and 1992 national school performance indicators showed 52 per cent of Year 11 students obtaining five or more A–C grades at GCSE. This had increasd to 57 per cent by 1994. Similarly, the response of students has been described as having many excellent features. The school's attendance rate in 1992 was 95 per cent; and unauthorised absences were 0.05 per cent. The school has a governing body of 19 and, at the time of our study, one vacancy.

A general inspection at Skelton by HMI took place in February 1991. The school was praised for the evidence of good and sometimes excellent work in most areas of the curriculum whereby students achieve high standards of learning and a good basis of knowledge and skills. The success of the school was attributed to the quality of its management, responsive students and a conscientious staff. Moreover, the school was said to be managing its resources well to promote effective learning: 'Skelton School has achieved considerable success in using its human and material resources to establish very good conditions for learning for its students.'

Our own sampling of the opinions of Year 9 students (83 per cent

Table 6.1 Attitudes to the school

What I think	strongly agree (%)	agree (%)	disagree (%)	strongly disagree (%)
I like coming to school	8.1	66.0	19.3	6.6
I am unhappy at school	4.0	6.6	53.0	36.4
My child likes coming to school	27.1	60.7	11.4	0.7
Most families support this school	26.4	70.0	2.1	1.4
My child is unhappy at school	2.1	5.7	50.0	42.1
I find school work interesting	5.9	59.7	26.9	7.5
I am often bored at school	13.8	40.0	39.0	7.2
My child finds school work interesting	15.0	67.9	14.3	2.9
Teachers in this school encourage me to do well	31.1	61.7	6.2	1.0
Teachers at this school don't encourage me enough in my work	1.0	9.8	64.4	24.7
I am made to feel welcome when I visit the school	35.0	56.4	6.4	2.1

response) and their parents (58 per cent response) showed their positive attitudes to the school and to the opportunities which it offered. We present these views in Table 6.1, organised into four sets of associated statements. In reporting these data, we also draw upon the additional written comments received; almost two-thirds of the students who replied used this opportunity to make additional comments.

In the first set of statements, we show that three-quarters of Year 9 students 'like coming to school' while just 10 per cent agreed with the statement 'I am unhappy at school'. These views are also reflected by parents, almost 88 per cent of those replying agreeing that 'My child likes coming to school' and fewer than 8 per cent believing their child is unhappy. One student wrote: 'The school is very nice. I'm proud to say I'm from this school. I like it most of the time.' A second student mentioned several features favourably: 'This school is brilliant. The teachers are nice and help you a lot. The school is clean and tidy and sets a high standard. Most topics are interesting or sometimes the teachers make it interesting. The school is excellent.'

Almost two-thirds of students agreed with the statement 'I find school work interesting' and 83 per cent of parents agreed with the comparable statement in their questionnaire. One student wrote: 'I like our school because there is always something to do. And I think most of the teachers are very good.' The role of teachers in contributing to this interest is caught by the comment 'The teachers in the school are very good at what they teach'. School work is not always interesting, however, just over half of the students agreeing with the statement 'I am often bored at school'. One example of this view is the comment: 'The school is OK but some work done is boring and not interesting'.

The third set of responses bring to the fore the importance of the support and encouragement offered by teachers. Almost 93 per cent of students at Skelton agree with the statement that 'Teachers in this school encourage me to do well' and 89 per cent disagree with the negative statement 'Teachers at this school don't encourage me enough in my work'. Several comments from the students reflect this response, as with: 'The facilities are excellent. Teachers give lots of encouragement'; and 'Nearly all the teachers are very caring and they help you a lot'. A third observed that 'The teachers don't look down on the students'.

This positive response is also reflected in the attitudes parents feel about the school's interest in them, over 91 per cent agreeing with the statement that 'I am made to feel welcome when I visit the school'. One comment identifies several strands in this perspective:

> The time my son has spent at Skelton High School has been a very happy time. This is all credit to the teaching staff who not only go out of their way to help the children with any problems they may have but are also very willing to speak to parents at any time. They always let you know if something is wrong and equally as quick to let you know if your child is doing well.

The data in Table 6.1, the written comments from parents and students, together with the quantitative indicators cited earlier, suggest that, in important respects, the school is 'getting it right'. This includes the way in which the school has spent its budget share on a number of projects, comments which we draw upon later. It is against this background and context that we turn to examine how the school has used its additional responsibilities for resources since becoming locally managed in April 1991.

RESOURCE USES AND THEIR OUTCOMES

Analysis of the information collected from the first phase visit to Skelton identified a number of projects initiated at the school as a result of local management. We termed these 'development projects' and they provided a starting point for the case study, since those interviewed were asked for their views on the suitability of these projects in meeting the needs of the school. We also asked them to identify other changes and their assessment of them. From these interviews a number of distinct strands of development are apparent and we have organised our account around four themes: staffing to meet needs, curriculum development, premises and accommodation, and student facilities.

Staffing to meet needs

Skelton shows how delegation has given senior managers a much greater sense of control. The deputy head compared the notion of curriculum control before LMS to the present arrangements:

> In theory curriculum analysis led to curriculum-led staffing but it's bunkum. Staffing was historical notwithstanding any plans put to the Authority. With LMS all-of-a-sudden this changed. Each year the curriculum analysis for the county was done and appeared to be ignored. In the first year of local management we realised we could do this. It was an SMT decision, then CPG for sounding and then sub-committee groups of governors; there are three relevant bodies.

The quotation also shows the process of consultation involved on this major issue. The overall balance of staffing depends upon a curriculum analysis which draws in heads of departments as well as the SMT and, because of the budgetary implications, also involves the governing body. The governing body has also used its discretion over salaries. One governor drew attention to the use of their powers in allocating 'salary resources to provide adequate reward for clerical staff, technicians, responsibilities for teaching staff'.

A further important manifestation of power at the school site are decisions not to replace a deputy head and a senior teacher. A review of the roles of the senior management was undertaken which included changes to the teaching loads of the two deputy heads who remain. The Chair of governors commented that

> Teaching loads have been re-arranged and greater responsibility given to other members of staff. I don't think of it from the financial point of view. I am very concerned about teaching and the education of students. It was possible to do it with one fewer deputy.

The school has appointed a senior teacher (resource and administration) and 1.6 extra staff in the office:

> We have top class administrative contributions to procedures and the presentation of materials. Our Senior Teacher keeps excellent records and [we have the] feel of being 'on top of' the situation. We know where we are which gives us the confidence to vire money around.
>
> (head teacher)

The benefit of this support for teaching and learning was set out by a head of department: 'There is no bottleneck in administration or reprographics which, under some circumstances, led to hasty, second rate lessons'.

Not only can the school decide its complement of staff, it can recruit early, a point made by one head of department:

> One of the benefits of LMS is the selection of candidates for jobs. We are no longer caught by redeployment and we can have a first grab at NQTs.

A head of faculty commented that it was now possible to move more quickly in advertising appointments and that this had led to better appointments. He described how this had allowed the school to appoint 'a number of very promising, able young teachers. They have injected enthusiasm and talent into the Faculty.' Another change is in the management of cover for absent teachers. It is now policy to employ supply cover after only one day. Before delegation, the school had been bound to the LEA's policy which required three days to pass before a replacement teacher could be employed. Using LM to meet the needs of the school is also apparent in curriculum development.

Curriculum development

Skelton is allocating funds to implement an 'information technology across the curriculum' (ITAC) policy. It is an area which was identified as a weakness in the HMI report and the school is using its powers of local management to allocate resources to improve provision. The school now has two information technology centres in each building which, the deputy head observed, 'would not have taken place without delegation'. The maths and the modern languages faculty each have a computer room alongside teaching rooms and the head of department's office; the accommodation for the humanities faculty is also being redesigned to give a comparable facility. The ITAC policy also acknowledges the need for staff development, and INSET funding is being used to support teachers in using these facilities. An extra technician has also been appointed whose primary responsibility is to support all departments in this area and in setting up audio-visual equipment for use in teaching. The overall purpose of the ITAC policy includes opportunities for students to explore a variety of simulation exercises in a range of curriculum settings and to develop database and word processing skills.

These developments are perceived by staff and governors as going some way to meeting curriculum needs. Members of the governing body did not feel able to comment on the impact of the development for student learning, although those whom we interviewed were aware of its priority: 'IT is certainly an area we need to put more resources into as it is one of the few areas in which this school is "weak"'. While governors were involved in the decisions on resource allocation – one governor interviewed was on the Premises Committee which had discussed the development – the project was 'essentially managed by the staff rather than governors'.

At all levels of staff there was an acknowledgement of the improved provision and its importance for student learning. One deputy took the view that the development 'has empowered staff to pass on relevant skills to students'. The heads of faculty of science and maths welcomed the increased access to technology; this was described as 'effective' in science and 'providing valuable support, advice and hardware to our Faculty and others'. Departmental staff, typically, were also positive: 'IT materials enable more time to be spent "doing" science rather than setting-up complicated equipment – so learning should be improved'. This positive view of IT was not universal: 'Some aspects may be good for students but English is affected by teaching too much "technology"'.

The importance of support for IT was evident in the comments of the technician. He observed that his job was changing in response to the needs of teachers and students: 'Only problem is that staff are unconfident about use of equipment . . . I am used more and more in the classroom for support – I love this – some other jobs have to take a back seat'. This view was also represented by one of the deputies: 'meets needs to some extent but takes a lot of staff training and confidence building – would not work if there was no technician'.

This example of curriculum development shows how the school has been able to use local management to respond to an area of recognised weakness. Physical, organisational and human resources have been harnessed to implement ITAC. That it remains a policy which is still at an early stage of implementation is reflected not only in some of the comments of staff but in the responses of parents and students. The responses in Table 6.2 show only 19 per cent of students agreeing with the

Table 6.2 IT facilities

What I think	strongly agree (%)	agree (%)	disagree (%)	strongly disagree (%)
I use computers in many different subjects	2.5	16.4	59.7	21.4
I hardly ever get to use computers at school	20.8	52.8	23.4	3.0
I use computers in my work more often than when I first came	6.0	21.4	48.8	23.8
My child hardly ever gets to use computers at school	23.7	37.8	35.6	3.0
There aren't enough computers at the school	16.4	35.8	41.0	6.7

statement that 'I use computers in many different subjects', a response which would reflect the gradual dissemination of IT through the Skelton curriculum.

Student responses to the other two statements may also be a measure of the early stages of policy implementation: over 70 per cent agreed with the statement 'I hardly ever get to use computers at school'; 30 per cent agreed with the statement 'I use computers in my work more often than when I first came'. Eleven students wrote additional comments on computers, all asking for more facilities and time.

Responses from parents show 60 per cent agreeing with the statement 'My child hardly ever gets to use computers at school' although opinion is more evenly divided as to whether the school has enough computers. Only three parents wrote an additional comment on computers, each suggesting a need for greater expenditure.

Taken together, these responses may well reflect the early stages of development of the ITAC policy. It may, however, also reflect a difference between expectations and what, in practice, can quickly be provided. Adding to IT facilities is expensive, so that a substantial commitment of resources by the school may still leave students and parents disappointed by the amount of IT time available for a single student; the more so in an area where the development of skills often leads to demands for greater access to time and equipment.

More modest but important allocations of resources had occurred elsewhere in the curriculum. Resourcing immediate needs was itemised by several staff. Earmarking resources for some of the minority languages was mentioned and provision of smaller classes to enable some students to do three sciences. Teachers also referred to an additional £600 per subject for books to meet requirements arising from the National Curriculum and one English teacher remarked on how funds were made available for 'emergencies', as in recent changes in the English curriculum. Student and parent responses to statements on books (Table 6.3) highlight

Table 6.3 Perspectives on books

What I think	strongly agree (%)	agree (%)	agree (%)	strongly disagree (%)
Often there are not enough books to go round	20.0	56.0	22.0	2.0
We get to use more new books than when I first came	7.1	43.9	46.4	2.6
Often there are not enough books to go round	14.9	44.8	38.8	1.5
The school buys a lot of new books	2.5	34.4	56.6	6.6

again the way in which delegated management can contribute to improvement. Three-quarters of students (59 per cent of parents) agreed with the statement 'Often there are not enough books to go round' but half of the students agreed with the statement 'We get to use more new books than when I first came'. Whether sufficient is spent on new books is doubted by some parents, 63 per cent disagreeing with the statement 'The school buys a lot of new books'.

Staff drew attention to the support for professional development and to the way incentive allowances had been used to support certain developments in the school. This included a report on how incentive allowances had been adapted to changing circumstances in one department. One science teacher observed that 'The staff salary bill has been reduced over the last few years by the appointment of younger staff'.

Premises and accommodation

Among developments to the premises, three were prominent from our first set of interviews: the covered walkway, the maths suite and the new science teaching rooms (Table 6.4). While there are differences of emphasis, these are all areas where there is a broad measure of agreement among staff, parents and students.

The covered walkway has been constructed between the main building and the second major teaching block. It is a wide and open space and is viewed by one governor as having a great potential for private lettings. Another suggested that it provided a better facility for students and has 'become a much utilised space'. A third governor expressed the view 'that it provides a physical link between the school buildings (commensurate with the ethos of the whole school) and is used as valuable space during curriculum evenings'.

That the walkway has improved the premises and 'made school life more comfortable and civilised' is the consensus among staff. One member of staff argued that it has a 'potential yet to be explored' and that it 'cuts down heating bills'. There does exist a degree of caution about the development, however, often expressed in terms of alternative use of the resources, as with the comment: 'expensive but useful – lots of other things more related to education more valued by me'.

Parents and students clearly support the development, more than 70 per cent of students and over 80 per cent of parents agreeing with the statement that 'The covered walkway is a great improvement to the school'. Fourteen students added written comments about the walkway and, despite the overall response to the attitude statement, 11 were of the view that the money could have been spent more wisely. Only one parent mentioned the walkway.

Table 6.4 Premises and accommodation

What I think	strongly agree (%)	agree (%)	disagree (%)	strongly disagree (%)
The covered walkway is a great improvement to the school	24.1	47.1	19.9	8.9
I do more interesting science work in the new science areas	11.0	43.5	38.7	6.8
The new maths and science rooms are excellent	2.1	43.0	44.0	10.9
The covered walkway is a great improvement to the school	32.1	49.6	13.1	5.1
The new maths and science rooms are excellent	9.4	54.7	32.1	3.8

The additional science rooms are not new laboratories but involved a more modest conversion of two existing classrooms in the vicinity of the main science accommodation. It has meant that trolleys with science equipment can be brought into the rooms and they can be used more easily for demonstrations. The changes in the maths faculty have included rearranging the use of rooms, providing separate space for computers and an office for the head of department. These are not major capital projects but represent the more modest but valuable opportunities available to schools when they are managing their own budgets.

Governors provided a shrewd assessment of these developments. One felt that the changes in the maths accommodation had 'been managed satisfactorily but is an inadequate solution to the problem caused by lack of LEA investment in school premises'. Another felt that changes to the science and maths accommodation made more effective use of the premises. One governor observed that one effect of the changes was that some students could now be taught in '"express" groups . . . More able children are taken out for higher level curriculum.'

The consensus among staff was that these changes were valuable. A head of department not benefiting directly from the change was positive about them: 'I have a sense of the need for Maths accommodation as I know they've been split up for some years'. Another head of department not directly affected commented that the 'developments have improved the delivery of academic quality that are growing in status and effectiveness within the school'. From within the science faculty came the view that 'for such a small sum of money spent, it has been relatively effective – nowhere near extra labs but one room is considerably better than a normal classroom . . . . Can do some limited practical work which otherwise could not have been done'. This view was not universal, one science teacher sceptical about the value of the change suggesting a 'minimal effect on students' learning'. From within the maths faculty, comment on the accommodation changes is positive. One teacher replied: 'The new IT facility for the use of mathematics is a great bonus – the classroom will take a full class of students .... Students have appreciated the maths computer room, they see it as a bonus to be taken there'; another summarised the changes as 'priority areas .... I feel that the SMT has managed the money extremely well'.

Table 6.4 suggests that students themselves take a positive view of what must generally be recognised as modest changes to the accommodation; 54 per cent of replies agreed with the statement 'I do more interesting science work in the new science areas'. That fewer than half of the students agreed with the statement 'The new maths and science rooms are excellent' may reflect an assessment that the changes may be good rather than excellent!

Accounts of development projects should not obscure the importance and significance of smaller scale initiatives. Invited to give examples of other ways in which the school has allocated resources to premises, governors and staff cited many instances. One governor reported that they had 'toured the school' and identified the need for better blinds in some rooms and improved insulation in others. The entrance to the school had been redecorated and carpeted, one governor noting that '"First impressions" are very important'. Changes to the lighting in the sports' hall were seen as benefiting students and providing an opportunity for increasing income from lettings.

These comments by governors found echoes in some of the remarks from the staff whom we interviewed. Enhancement to the premises also found favour among staff. One comment summarised how carpeting had resulted in a 'good atmosphere, quiet, enables us to do drama/movement work, sit on the floor etc.'. Others also drew attention to minor but valuable improvements in premises, decoration and furnishings, leading to this summary from one senior teacher: 'Since LMS the environment and facilities of the school have improved dramatically. I believe we are using our independence very well.' Students and parents were asked to respond to a range of statements on the school environment. Responses in Table 6.5 to statements on the state of decoration suggest that this is an area where improvement is occurring. While 45 per cent of students (and 33 per cent of parents) agree with the statement 'The school needs decorating', about 80 per cent of students and parents agree that the inside of the school is 'better decorated' than it used to be; 72 per cent of students agreed that 'The corridors and classrooms look nicer than when I first came'. Asked whether 'The school is in a poor state of repair', 95 per cent of parents disagreed.

Table 6.5 The state of the fabric

What I think	strongly agree (%)	agree (%)	disagree (%)	strongly disagree (%)
The school needs decorating	12.1	33.3	46.0	8.6
The inside of the school is better decorated than when I first came	20.4	59.7	15.4	4.5
The corridors and classrooms look nicer than when I first came	9.5	62.3	24.1	4.0
A well-decorated classroom makes me want to work harder	4.0	33.2	48.2	14.6
The school needs decorating	3.6	29.2	57.7	9.5
Rooms and corridors are better decorated than they used to be	11.4	70.5	17.4	0.8
The school is in a poor state of repair	0.7	4.3	71.9	23.0

Work on premises is an important component of the use schools generally – as well as Skelton in particular – have made of their delegated powers. Intuitively, this makes good sense and many would agree that a good physical environment is a contributory factor to learning. Since testing this intuitive judgement is less commonplace, we asked students to respond to the statement, 'A well-decorated classroom makes me want to work harder': 37 per cent of students agreed with the statement and 53 per cent disagreed. It is a result which may suggest that the work of a large minority may be affected by the state of classroom decoration, while others appear to be less susceptible to this factor. The outcome provides some support for the greater attention to the physical environment which appears to be one aspect of delegated management, although it offers little guidance on how much resources and attention compared with other needs. Our data in this area also offer some evidence on student priorities, a great many of the additional comments drawing attention to the state of the toilets at Skelton.

Student facilities

Several of the governors and staff reported the introduction of storage lockers for students and, for PE, separate shower cubicles as a means of improving students' quality of life. One member of staff commented that the lockers had 'reduced crush in corridors – given students a "home" – improved image . . . . Overall they have had a very positive effect on life in school and improved image and atmosphere.' These remarks were typical of the comments we received from staff about the lockers. The showers attracted less universal support but one reply may reflect an insight into the student perspective: 'Initially it seemed a little strange but on reflection there probably was a real need which has been met here – life is much more pleasant for students'. One teacher gave a useful summary of the benefits: 'the projects have affected the students' general well-being which makes school a more positive experience for them'.

The student and parent responses in Table 6.6 certainly show enthusiasm for the lockers, almost 90 per cent of students, and over 90 per cent of parents, agreeing with the statement 'I think the lockers were a good idea'. In responding to the statement 'I used to dislike games and PE because of the showers', replies from 24 per cent of students suggest that the changes to the shower arrangements were welcomed and may have affected their attitude to PE. Further analysis showed a statistically significant gender difference in the responses: while 36 per cent of girls agreed with the statement, only 5 per cent of boys did so.

We conclude this part of our account with some general comments which highlight the views of staff on the effect of delegated management. One head of department reported that 'The school seems to have spent the money usefully on projects which have been of benefit to both students and staff. It certainly has not been wasted even though I'm sure there has been disagreement over priorities'. A less senior member of staff wrote:

> School is able to focus on particular needs/requirements and deal with them more rapidly. This includes fabric of the building/resources/ curriculum concerns. There is more a feel of 'this is our school' (this can lead to insularity, of course).

How decision-making processes have contributed to these circumstances and views is a theme of the next section.

Table 6.6 Student facilities

What I think	strongly agree (%)	agree (%)	disagree (%)	strongly disagree (%)
I think the lockers were a good idea	45.8	42.3	8.5	3.5
I used to dislike games and PE because of the showers	9.0	15.6	49.2	26.1
I think the lockers were a good idea	56.7	35.5	5.0	2.8

RESOURCE MANAGEMENT

Using resources to their best effect means ensuring that the needs of students in classrooms are met. Understanding how that link is established at Skelton is the theme of this section. We begin with a summary of the formal committee structure of the school, its membership and cycle of meetings. This is followed by an account of the processes of development planning at the school which, our interview record suggests, occupies a central role in linking resources to curriculum priorities. The plan as a published document distinguishes between whole school issues and those which are specific to faculties and departments, parts of the school which have a key role in organising teachers into groups as well as being a link to the school as a whole. How these parts of the school work must, therefore, be an essential component for understanding the linkages between resources and learning.

The structure of decision making

The apex of decision making in the school is the governing body. At the time of our study, the governing body had 19 members, including one vacancy. There is a full meeting of the governing body twice each term. Much of its work has been delegated to smaller groups which, typically, also meet twice a term. Two of these groups – Finance and Staffing – are designated as sub-committees. The school's prospectus notes that

> With the advice of the Head Teacher, who is responsible for the day-to-day management, our Finance Sub-Committee determines priorities on how money should be spent .... The Staffing Sub-Committee is responsible for deciding staffing levels and the Chairman is involved in interviews for the appointment of senior members of staff.

There are also two permanent working parties. A Premises Working Party has a responsibility for checking the condition of school buildings and grounds; a Curriculum Working Party includes membership from governors and teaching staff and has a responsibility for monitoring and evaluating the curriculum. The importance of resource management for this governing body is reflected in the remarks of the Chairman in the prospectus: 'In the main the greater powers which have been given to the Governors are in order to direct resources to the needs of the School and make the School more responsive to the educational needs of its students'.

Separate to the governing body and its committees are a set of meetings and committees whose membership is almost exclusively made up of teachers. There are six permanent groups where staff meet: staff meetings, Curriculum Policy Group (CPG), Heads of Year, faculty meetings, departmental meetings and Year team meetings. All of these bodies meet one week in six, so that in a half term each would meet once and there would be one week where none met.

The staff meeting is the only group which brings together all teachers and it can also include members of the support staff. CPG is the main curriculum group in the school whose membership includes: a head teacher and two deputies, heads of faculty and the cross-curricular co-ordinators. Pastoral matters are discussed in a parallel committee whose membership includes the deputy responsible for pastoral matters, five heads of year, the Special Needs Curriculum Co-ordinator and a represent-ative from the Behaviour Support Service. CPG and the Pastoral Group meet together for one in three of their meetings. While CPG and the Pastoral Group are the permanent whole school committees, working groups are constituted to address specific problems and are then wound up. Faculty meetings are where heads of faculty meet members of their faculty and, if faculties include departments, these also meet one week in six. Faculties and departments are curriculum units while meetings of Year teams provide opportunities for staff to discuss issues specific to pastoral matters. It is the policy of the school that minutes are recorded for all these meetings and these are sent to the head teacher.

There is a seventh committee responsible for whole school issues. This is the Senior Management Team (SMT) which consists of the head teacher and his two deputies. The SMT meets twice weekly: once after school for an hour and a half and once during the school day for the same length of time.

Clearly, the members are the dynamic which causes formal structures to function and, as we shall report, the three members of the SMT are central to that, not least because they provide the linkages across the structure. There are, however, other important connecting strands, includ-ing the heads of faculty. It also became evident that development planning contributes to the processes linking resources to student learning.

The Development Plan at Skelton

Guidance from the DFEE and a good deal of advice in the training literature argues that development planning is the means by which resources can be harnessed to the learning needs of students and the priorities of the school. Our interviews at Skelton suggest that for many staff, development planning is an activity of which they are well aware and in which they participate. The structure of Skelton's published Development Plan pro-vides a useful first step in understanding the processes which lie behind its preparation.

As a statement of resource allocation, the nine pages of the Development Plan have three distinct parts. The first part sets the context with a statement of school aims followed by information on the budget, school roll and brief reference to major new developments; these include items such as teacher appraisal and expected changes to the National Curriculum. Despite the information that the school budget is £2,060,000, the plan itself refers to the allocation of only about £80,000. Why this should be so becomes apparent in the presentation of the information.

The main body of the plan is set out in nine sections – Curriculum, Pastoral, Assessment, Special Needs, Staff Development and INSET, Staff, Premises and Buildings, Resources, and Community – but, from a resource allocation perspective, these are of two main kinds. There are some sections which are of major significance for the use of staff time but their financial and staffing implications are not set out. The section on the curriculum is a striking example. It contains statements on subject priorities in the forthcoming year but no reference to their resource implications. Later in the plan there is a three-line item which notes the *change* in staffing levels for the coming year: 'An increase in staffing from 1.9.92 will allow for extra time for Special Needs, Religious Studies, Maths and English. This should be no more than 1.3 staff.' In other words, the section which earmarks most of the school's budget makes almost no reference to finance. That this should be so reflects the focus of the document, listing curriculum priorities as the work to be done. It is clear from our interview data, moreover, that the financial implications of staffing the curriculum are thoroughly calculated. By contrast to this absence of financial information on the curriculum, there are five sections where a cost is provided against several proposed developments. Many of these costed items refer to changes which will affect the school as a whole, a difference which provides a clue to key features of decision making and development planning at Skelton.

Processes of whole school management

If we are to understand decision making at Skelton, we must begin with the Head and meetings of the Senior Management Team (SMT). An extended extract from an interview (interviewer, I) with the Head (H) gives some insight into how it works and its influence in the school. It also gives his perspective on the inter-relationships between different committees:

H: We have meetings on Monday morning . . . and an agenda is drawn up. Nine times out of ten it's drawn up by me but it includes items that are put on the agenda by the others, at the previous meeting . . . [telephone interrupts] . . . items that they raise and that I want to put on, and we just discuss them through and then make some decisions based on those. That's loosely how it works.

I: That could lead you to taking things to CPG or Pastoral or whatever.

H: Yes, yes, and deciding, for example, on things like a staff development policy, which is a most recent thing. One of the deputies presented a paper on a staff development policy and, at the meeting, we decided we would do it in a different way. We are going to be part of *Investors in People* and so we decided we would link the objectives of *Investors in People* with our staff development policy . . . one of them will write the staff development policy, we will discuss it here together, then we will go to the wider group and say: this is what we are proposing, how does this seem?

We've just done the same with the spelling policy. We've just done the same with a marking policy. With the spelling policy, we had it written, we discussed it here, went through it in great detail with the person who wrote it, then had a staff meeting session on it and said: this is the policy we are proposing, are there any faults with it, problems with it? Shared it amongst them, agreed it, then, at the next CPG meeting we said: there's the policy, how are we going to implement it? What does this mean in the classroom, what does it mean for your faculty? . . . It's got to get out where the people are and the only way to do that is to go through the channels and say: now, that's what's going to happen. The next thing is if it doesn't happen, we go to see . . . and say why hasn't it happened? We agreed it, we talked about it, you knew about it, that's what we said we would do.

I: May I just ask where the initiatives for the spelling policy and marking policy came from?

H: The spelling policy came from us, the senior management. The marking policy initiative came out of the CPG because it was argued that every faculty has a different policy . . . we set up a working party to look at that, who made recommendations to the CPG.

The extract illustrates the way in which the SMT acts both as an *initiator* of developments and as a *supporter* of proposals made by others. This readiness to support ideas from others assists us in understanding why, elsewhere in the interview, the head teacher describes CPG and the heads of year meetings as key committees and why, moreover, similar views were expressed in other interviews, as in this comment from an allowance holder:

Having joined Skelton from a school where staff were ill-informed and had little influence on decision-making, I appreciate the opportunities that we do have in all aspects of running the school. The SMT do listen and I am quite aware of whole school priorities most of the time.

This dual role of the SMT is important in understanding why our interviews with staff convey an impression of clear leadership from the senior management *and* a sense of involvement. The direction and decision making associated with leadership is apparent in the *initiating* role of the

SMT but their readiness to *support* ideas and suggestions from others reflects an approach which involves others. With respect specifically to the management of resources, this duality of leadership-as-initiating and involvement-as-supporting is present in the *process* of preparing the Development Plan.

The annual cycle begins in the summer with a faculty review which leads to papers going to the SMT in late October 'in order to build this into the next year's financial position' (head teacher). These papers set out requirements for staffing and other resource needs of each faculty and are discussed by the SMT before being reworked by the head teacher and the finance manager into a form where they go to the finance sub-committee of the governing body. In addition to these faculty requirements, there are activities which are not specific to a faculty. According to the head teacher, decision making in these two areas differ.

Priorities as between faculties are decided by the SMT, on the grounds that only they have an overview:

> It's very difficult to get people to take the wide view when they are working in the English faculty or the maths faculty so, on specifics like that, we take the overview because we say we are the only ones who can realistically be expected to.

Where there are proposals for expenditure on whole school items, there is a voting procedure: 'we write them a long list and put them out to staff and say, vote on it . . . . They hand the sheets in, we then count up the votes . . . . it's one of the few things we operate in that particular way'. The list on which staff are asked to vote is compiled from three main sources: a survey of staff which asks for their suggestions, items extracted from the Faculty Reviews because they are defined as whole school (such as decorating corridors outside classrooms) as well as suggestions made by the SMT. In 1992–3, the total cost of the items from the school list which were included in the plan was about £100,000.

These processes, and their importance for preparing the plan, emerge in many of our interviews. We asked how resource needs and priorities were identified for the whole school and what their understanding was of their role in decision making. Twelve out of 15 members of the teaching staff whom we interviewed made a significant reference to the Development Plan or to processes clearly related to its preparation. Their comments also convey their perceptions as to the participatory nature of decision making in the school.

According to one standard scale maths teacher, 'Each year, the School Development Plan. As part of a staff meeting, staff split into groups – either interest or arbitrarily – to discuss items to be included, could be anything . . . . Then head teacher reports back with pricing and budget'. She felt able to influence decisions 'to the extent that I can pass on any ideas or concerns through different channels' and added that 'most working parties are open to anyone'.

The balance between 'initiating' and 'supporting' is not easy to maintain and does not satisfy everyone. In an interview which expressed some concerns about the nature and adequacy of consultation, one allowance holder said that 'The SMT could be too decisive'. Another allowance holder wrote that she did not feel that she had much influence on whole school issues while also noting: 'I do have a voice, however, and feel I can express my views'. It is the comment of one head of department which catches the sense of balance:

> I have a sense of being involved and I feel sufficiently well informed. It is important that I am only involved in issues where I have a real say and not put through pointless consultation exercises, involving issues that are really the responsibility of a management team that have already formed conclusions. The balance seems right to me.

Decisions on resources by the governing body also exhibit the initiating role of the SMT. A parent governor reported how proposals which came to the finance sub-committee were usually accepted and went on to emphasise that it was the job of 'day-to-day' management to suggest criteria by which resource choices could be prioritised. A second parent governor did not feel that they were 'rubber-stamps':

> I do feel that if governors are to play a full and active role in the life of the school they must be involved in the decision process. This is not to deny the vital role of the head teacher and SMT in the day-to-day management of the school.

For the head teacher, this means making firm proposals to the finance sub-committee. If a proposal is made to the Head, in recommending it to finance, 'They would expect me to know where it [the money] might come from and they would not [otherwise] expect me to come to them . . . . So, there's a certain amount of autonomy.'

In the context of a planning cycle, the resource implications of the faculty review and the Development Plan lead into the budget proposals which are made in March. This is done by the head teacher and the finance manager:

> We cost the salaries . . . and we allocate a recommendation in every other sub-heading to take into account the recommendations insofar as we are able, and then we put it to the governing body (the Finance sub-committee) and we talk them through it line by line; why we've done what we've done. Nothing's been changed. They accept that almost as it is and they are, so far, reasonably complimentary. But we do face them with the hard decisions. This is what we are doing, this is why we are

doing it, this is what it means, these are the implications; are you happy with that?

Subsequently there are regular briefing meetings on the financial report and an opportunity to propose changes although, below £1,500, the head teacher has the authority to proceed.

How these decisions on the budget become good quality experiences for students depends not only upon the leadership of the school as a whole but upon the way teachers work together within faculties and departments. It is to those parts of the school to which we now turn.

Processes of resource management in faculties and departments

Teachers and support staff were interviewed from several departments and faculties: English, maths, science, languages, technology and history. In addition, we attended departmental meetings in English, maths, science and Year meetings for tutors in Years 9 and 11.

In one of the main subject areas, those whom we interviewed about resource management mentioned informal conversation and meetings as key elements of the process. They also said that decisions about items such as books were often determined by the requirements of the National Curriculum. One member of a department suggested that roles in decision making could be 'as great or as little as each individual desires – the management style is very open and invites views and discussion'. Another indicated that the views of teachers were valued. Our observations of a meeting of the department exhibited these features.

A member of staff in another major subject area observed that 'Departmental needs are discussed with Faculty teams and bids made to SMT for consideration'. At the departmental meeting which we attended, agenda items included expenditure on learning materials and the allocation of in-service training. Most members of staff contributed during the course of a meeting. It was chaired firmly and the group were led through a substantial agenda, ensuring that decisions were made where they were required.

In a third department, staff interviews showed that informal as well as formal conversation contributed to the assessment of resource requirements. One newly qualified teacher wrote: 'Needs identified by staff passed on to head of faculty who makes a decision based on concerns and opinion of faculty members'. Another described the process in much the same way, adding: 'This system is efficient when the decision is within the faculty'. The faculty meeting followed an agenda prepared in advance and, while the head of faculty led much of the discussion, others contributed and on some items took the lead.

Across departments, there was evidence of information flowing between departments and the management of the school as a whole. This was a two-way process and reinforced our view that ideas about resource requirements came from among the staff as well as from senior management initiatives.

CONCLUSION: INITIATING AND SUPPORTING IMPROVEMENT

The case study of Skelton is a reminder of how we must not underestimate the purposefulness of a head teacher. Under his leadership, the school has grasped the opportunity offered by local management and largely fitted this into existing structures and processes. A comment on the change to LMS by one well-established but not senior allowance holder is indicative: 'I would say that the impression is that the school was efficiently managed [before] and that the change has had little effect that has been noticeable. This obviously is a good indication for how the school is managed.' The quality of that management, certainly as embodied in the head teacher, is a view shared by parents. Table 6.7 shows 91 per cent of parents agreeing with the statement 'The school is well led by the head teacher'.

A head teacher alone has only limited effect, however, and Skelton also benefits from its active governing body and its staff. Middle managers appear to provide leadership within faculties and departments which complement the whole school leadership of the Head and SMT. They have the benefit of working with a staff who are committed to their tasks. In some important respects, the capacity of the school effectively to link resources to learning is summarised by one of the teachers: 'I feel all Skelton staff are very professional and we are encouraged by SMT to take part in the planning of the school's requirements'.

These attributes are important aspects of those associated with an effective school and, at the beginning of this chapter, we cited the positive comments about teaching and learning, made by HMI in its inspection in February 1991. The same report commented upon the school's 'considerable success in using its human and material resources to establish very good conditions for learning for its students'. On the basis of our own observations, we would concur with these comments and their implication that Skelton is cost-effective in its use of resources. In this closing section, we will reflect on our case study for evidence of characteristics we suggest are associated with the cost-effective school.

Table 6.7 The leadership of the head teacher

What I think	strongly agree (%)	agree (%)	disagree (%)	strongly disagree (%)
The school is well led by the head teacher	39.4	51.8	7.3	1.5

The case study of Skelton shows evidence of some degree of *radical audit*. Decisions not to replace a deputy head teacher and a senior teacher, changes in administrative structures, reorganisations of premises into departmental suites, alterations of buildings to create new rooms, are examples of decisions which would not have occurred without the opportunity provided by local management. Development of the premises is a good example of how delegated responsibility encourages schools to be creative and appraise the use of a resource in ways they would not previously have done.

Information on *costs* at Skelton is not cost-centred in a conventional sense, although budgets to departments for learning materials are available in cost-centre format with authorisation also delegated. Information on other resources is available in a variety of forms. Staffing needs, for example, are decided following a curriculum analysis and this provides a profile of the departmental allocation of teachers. This analysis takes lesson periods as the unit of account. This is a different way of measuring resources as compared with the use of money for allocating the budget for learning materials. Most financial information is presented in the traditional line budget and this is carefully monitored and presented, enabling the school to consider options and 'vire money around'. It is also clear that financial planning is good. For example, the senior teacher (resource and administration) prepares budget projections to inform judgements of budget priorities. The budget statement itself is contained in the Development Plan. Other sections of the plan also contain priorities for the coming year but in the section which shows the staff dispositions for the coming year, no reference is made to their financial cost. Whether these different approaches to the presentation of resources are sufficient for informing cost-effective decisions is a theme to which we will return in our closing chapters.

The school has good systems of *internal delegation*. Our observations of departmental meetings and our interview data provide evidence of teaching staff participating in decisions close to their own areas of expertise. These include decisions on learning materials and professional development but they can also include small scale staffing options, the overall structure of staffing being a matter for whole school decision. This approach reflects the head teacher's view that 'it's very difficult to get people to take the wide view when they are working in the English faculty or the maths faculty', so that the SMT must make proposals on whole school issues.

This does not mean that staff have no opportunities for participating in discussions and decisions on whole school issues, the school having an extensive structure of decision making for enabling a *dialogue of accountability*. We have described the network of committees with task groups established to examine any special issues. This structure functions in ways which strike a balance between change being *initiated* by the head teacher and the SMT and this leadership *supporting* ideas that come from others, examples of each being the development of policies on spelling and marking. In this balance, we should not underestimate the decisive leadership provided by the head teacher and the SMT but no more should we ignore the role of the committees as a means by which proposals can be identified, considered and reviewed. All the key interests are represented in the decision structure with the head teacher and the SMT providing the members common to governor committees and professional committees. It is also clear that the process of development planning is clearly recognised in the school and different groups recognise roles in the process.

As with Broome School, this decision-making structure provides information *for* management as well as being a means whereby management *tells* others what is going to happen. In this respect, the opportunity to receive information is a way by which dangers of the *detachment of management* can be minimised. The school uses a staff survey to collect views about whole school priorities and information on the quality of learning is assessed by senior management looking at the work produced by students. Our interview and survey data suggest that the policies and priorities of the school are consistent with the assessments of teachers, students and parents, suggesting that management at Skelton is well informed about needs and priorities.

Whether enough of the sources of information available are sufficiently *independent* of the head teacher and teachers is less clear. The level of satisfaction reported in the interview and survey data points to a school which is 'getting it right', not only in making decisions about its educational priorities but in how it arrives at these decisions. This is strong *prima facie* evidence that all is well and we would not contest that specific point. Moreover, there is evidence of the head teacher collecting information on student performance which is independent of the teachers. Our concern is whether governors, in particular, have access to information which is independent of the head teacher and fellow teachers. This is a general issue and not one specific to Skelton and is one we consider in the closing chapter.

What is evident from the whole approach at Skelton is that it is a school that is meeting educational needs well and using its resources to good effect, a view captured by two students in their comments: 'The facilities are excellent. Teachers give lots of encouragement'; and: 'Nearly all the teachers are very caring and they help you a lot'.

Chapter 7

Whittaker School

Challenging and leading

A VIEW OF THE SCHOOL

Whittaker School is a grant maintained 12–18 mixed comprehensive serving a county town and surrounding villages. In 1993 the standard number was 244 and the number on roll 1,094 with 165 pupils in the sixth form. There are other LEA comprehensive schools in the vicinity and a large independent school nearby. The school has been admitting above its standard number and remains oversubscribed, although the overall number of pupils has declined: 263 were admitted in September 1992, 260 in September 1993 and 248 in September 1994.

The teaching staff complement for 1993–4 was 68, including the head teacher, and represents an increase on the previous two years (1991–2: 65.3 and 1992–3: 66.2). For the academic year 1992–3 the school had a non-teaching staff of 22. The school has a full complement of governors on a governing body of 20.

Whittaker School takes its pupils from over 20 local middle schools and a high proportion come from outside the traditional catchment area. The intake comprises pupils from a wide socio-economic spectrum and 20 per cent come from ethnic minority groups, mainly Asian. The school has one statemented pupil for special needs support and a small proportion (57 pupils) are entitled to free school meals.

The school has been locally managed since April 1990 and was granted grant maintained status in April 1992. In 1992–3 the school's annual maintenance grant was £2.2m. Total annual income amounted to £2.4m after additional central government grants, including capital grants. For 1993–4 the annual maintenance grant is £2.39m with total income, including government grants, of £2.98m. One of the most obvious benefits of grant maintained status, thus far, is the extra capital funding which has been made available for a new technology building and the school is working on a long term strategy for future capital expenditure. Since the appointment of a new head teacher in 1991 and the change to grant maintained status, the school has rapidly developed new management structures.

Students at Whittaker School continue to enjoy success in public examinations. In 1992 the school offered 23 subjects at GCSE and 20 subjects at A-level. In addition some AS-level and business studies courses are offered to the sixth form; 39.1 per cent of Year 11 pupils achieved five or more grades A–C at GCSE and 96.4 per cent five or more grades A–G. These percentages are above the national average of 38 per cent and 82 per cent respectively. In 1994, 50 per cent of pupils at the school achieved five or more A–C grades at GCSE. At A/AS-level in 1992, 58 pupils were entered for one or more A/AS-level examinations achieving an average score of 19.1 points per candidate. This is well above the national average of 14.6 points per pupil. Pupil destinations at age 16+ show that nearly all pupils continue their education either at school (46.4 per cent in 1993) or at local colleges of further education (41.2 per cent in 1993). Less than 10 per cent went on to other training schemes in 1993 with 2.3 per cent finding employment. On leaving the sixth form the majority of students go on to university degree courses including those at Oxford and Cambridge.

The school is fortunate in the support it receives from parents and the local business community. If parents are more prominent than the business community in their financial support, the latter give significant support to careers education. The school has not been notably active in seeking external funds from either of these sources and, indeed, would not appear to have benefited greatly from external financial assistance. As with Broome and Skelton, a survey of Year 9 parents (45 per cent response) and pupils (85 per cent response) was undertaken as part of the study. Table 7.1 shows 90 per cent of parents agreed with the statement 'Most families support this school' and 95 per cent agreed with the statement 'My child likes coming to school'. Only 5 per cent agreed with the statement 'My child is unhappy at school' and one parent described the school as 'one of the most reputable schools in the area'. These responses reinforce the claims made that the school has been a popular choice with local parents for some time.

Pupils endorse these high satisfaction levels. Table 7.2 shows that 76 per cent agreed with the statement 'I liked coming to school' and only 10 per cent agreed with the statement 'I am unhappy at school'.

Table 7.1 Year 9 parents: Whittaker School

What I think	strongly agree (%)	agree (%)	disagree (%)	strongly disagree (%)
My child likes coming to school	23.5	71.3	4.3	0.9
Most families support this school	15.8	73.7	9.6	0.9
My child is unhappy at school	0.9	4.3	56.9	37.9

Table 7.2 Year 9 pupils: Whittaker School

What I think	strongly agree (%)	agree (%)	disagree (%)	strongly disagree (%)
I like coming to school	2.8	73.3	19.8	4.1
I am unhappy at school	3.6	5.9	59.5	30.9

Attitudes towards the school environment and its facilities were also tested with pupils and parents and these are included in later sections of the chapter. We also examine how the school has managed the change to grant maintained status at the same time as adjusting to a new head teacher.

RESOURCE USE AND OUTCOMES

Whittaker School has enhanced physical and human resources since gaining grant maintained status. The extra funding made available to the school has been a factor in enabling certain developments to take place. This has meant small but significant change to the premises and enhancement of human and physical support for teaching and learning.

Improving the school environment

Dating from the 1950s, the school buildings have been well looked after. However, under local management the furniture budget had been cut by the local authority and, in the view of one member of staff, nothing had really been done, so far as premises were concerned, for 30 years. Under local management the school libraries had been reorganised. As a result a larger library, previously reserved for sixth formers only, became a resource for the whole school and a smaller library became the sixth form study area. Such refurbishment as was necessary was funded from the school budget with some external assistance from local industry. This reorganisation was generally greeted with approval by staff, pupils and parents in redressing the balance of library provision to meet better the needs of the school. One member of staff felt that this 'considerable improvement' now invites pupils rather than repels them.

Since grant maintained status was obtained, however, Whittaker School has initiated a five-year rolling programme for refurbishment of premises with decisions on priority areas designed to take account of staff and pupil needs. Transitional grant maintained funding was already being used to refurbish office areas, pupil toilet areas and to create a new marking area for staff. Several members of staff described these as welcome developments and a big boost to morale. It was generally appreciated and identified as one of the tangible benefits of grant maintained status.

Governors also recognised the importance of improvements such as this: 'Improvements to morale of staff in spite of many pressures.'

The availability of an annual minor capital works fund and major capital grants – to which the school has made bids for premises modernisation – is a significant factor in enabling the planned rolling programme. Thus the school has plans for refurbishment of cloakroom areas and the development of a business studies area to facilitate sixth form vocational courses. Major capital grants have been awarded for a new technology block, the building of which has just begun, and further bids were planned for other departments. The School Buildings Committee was working towards a long-term plan of curriculum suites and future capital bids would be tailored accordingly. It should be noted, however, that while the availability of such funding in principle was seen as an opportunity by the school to plan ahead, such funds were earmarked and subject to DFE approval year on year.

It was recognised that premises' refurbishments on a smaller scale had already been carried out and these were seen as significant. In addition to those mentioned, carpets in teaching rooms, some new furniture and extra blinds all improve the learning environment. These improvements have had an immediate impact and one member of staff commented: 'The most obvious change has been premises refurbishment including the staff marking area – these were vital and resources seem to have been managed well.' Another teacher remarked: 'The carpets in teaching rooms have improved the environment in which pupils work – quieter, more civilised and appreciated by both staff and pupils.'

Some members of staff doubted the impact of refurbishment on pupils but our survey of Year 9 pupils and their parents (see Tables 7.3 and 7.4) revealed their satisfaction with the state of repair and decoration at the school: 92 per cent of pupils agreed that 'carpets in the classroom are a great improvement' and 78 per cent agreed that 'The inside of the school is better decorated than when I first came'.

Table 7.3 Year 9 pupils: Whittaker School

What I think	strongly agree (%)	agree (%)	disagree (%)	strongly disagree (%)
A well-decorated classroom makes me want to work harder	4.5	38.3	50.0	7.2
The inside of the school is better decorated than when I first came	8.6	68.5	22.1	0.9
Carpets in the classroom are a great improvement	35.1	56.8	7.2	0.9

Table 7.4 Year 9 parents: Whittaker School

What I think	strongly agree (%)	agree (%)	disagree (%)	
The school is in a poor state of repair	1.8	5.3	73.7	
Rooms and corridors are better decorated than they used to be	3.7	68.2	25.2	2.8

Parents also expressed satisfaction with the school environment: 'Now that the school is grant maintained there has been a distinct improvement in the amount of money being invested in the infrastructure of the school'. Only 7 per cent agreed that the school is in a poor state of repair and 72 per cent felt that rooms and corridors are better decorated than they used to be. When invited to make additional comments, many pupils did comment on the state of decoration of the school, several pointing out inadequacies in toilet facilities and furnishings in teaching rooms. One recognised the benefits but expressed concern about other areas:

> I think the school is better off since we became grant maintained, and much more of the school has been decorated i.e. carpets in most of the rooms, new tables and chairs. We also now have a drinks machine and hand dryers in the toilets, which the school didn't have when I first came. I think that the toilets need improving though I think these should be redecorated. I think there should be better bike sheds as they [the bikes] keep getting stolen.

For several pupils, grant maintained status seemed to equate with extra funds and some of them questioned the use of such funds for decorations when they felt there was a need for extra books and equipment:

> The school seems to have a lot more money now but a lot of it appears to go on painting and decorating rooms and corridors. Although more money is available for the school it doesn't seem to go on the right things like books and equipment. Having said that, the school did need to be decorated in parts and it has been improved.

Curriculum materials

Since local management in 1990 the school has allocated more funds to departments for curriculum materials and equipment. In the first year of LMS it is estimated that the school increased this funding – traditionally known as the capitation budget – by 30 per cent. At the same time, a new system of devolved funding to departments was introduced, a formula allocation based on the number of pupils and teaching sessions per subject. This is a more open system than previously operated as all staff can see the formula for all departments. The deputy head who introduced the system is satisfied that staff have welcomed the change: 'Even those departments who were losing were happy with the new open system and it has not been changed since.' Since grant maintained status the money for departments has been increased again, still out of annual budget, by a 100 per cent increase on the pre-grant maintained figure. In addition a special purposes grant of £20,000 is available into which departments may bid for curriculum innovation and development, in line with their departmental development plans.

Staff reaction to increased resources would, however, appear to be muted. While senior management recognised that 'money put into capitation is essential to meet the demands of the national curriculum' one head of department confesses that the changes have not 'had the impact I might have hoped for, but some improvement'. It seems to be the case that grant maintained status has raised expectations of staff for increased support for materials and equipment and it may also be the case that the current system still has anomalies which need addressing. In particular some departments feel that the element for day-to-day consumables for practical subjects (exacerbated by the payment of VAT) is inadequate. Others expressed concern about the inadequate element for fixed costs. However, it may just be the case that the school is having to meet expectations raised from a previously low base. As one governor put it: 'Capitation has increased but more needs to be done as finance becomes available to purchase equipment to reduce deficiencies resulting from earlier underfunding.' That being so, some staff make the point that extra funding in this area is hardly a bonus: 'I don't see how we could have coped (with national curriculum requirements)'. Indeed the large increases in funding have not been felt by some: 'There has been a marginal increase in capitation over the years – but not a major impact – I am still crossing out orders due to lack of funding.'

It is not evident that the special purposes grant is being well used by departments, possibly due to the immaturity of their planning processes or because some are not adequately informed. None of the staff to whom we spoke referred to it specifically. However, we were told that extra capitation had been made available for new National Curriculum set texts, books and computer resources. The physics department had been allocated curriculum development money for portable computers and the home economics department had additional funding to replace a fridge and a washing machine. Such small scale assistance is often of much significance for the teaching environment as one ancillary member of staff acknowledged: 'In my area money has been allocated for books, fume cupboards and ventilation systems. These are things we have asked for for several years. So being GM has allowed the management to spend money more effectively.'

While funding for curriculum materials provides staff with necessary learning materials which have direct implications for the teaching process, the impact of increased funding on pupil learning is less easy to assess. While the majority of Year 9 pupils (83 per cent) and parents (63 per cent) agreed that often there are not enough books to go round, there was more general agreement on the use of computers. For example, 63 per cent of parents disagreed with the statement 'There aren't enough computers at the school' and 57 per cent of pupils disagreed with the statement 'I hardly ever get to use computers at school'. However, as the previous pupil statements indicate, despite increased funding, there remains dissatisfaction and expectations of what should be provided in curriculum materials and equipment.

Human resources

Increased funding targeted at teaching and support staff appears to have had a notable impact on the school's development. Two initiatives, in particular, have had positive effects: the delegation of an increased professional development budget to departments and the appointment of a school administrator.

As a grant maintained school, Whittaker receives a development grant of £42.00 per pupil which includes funding for staff development. This amounted to £24,000 in 1992–3 for in-service training of staff. The school has handled this fund by allocating responsibility to one of the deputy head teachers who works with a Staff Development Committee (formerly the In-service Training Committee) which comprises representatives from all faculties. The budget is devolved to departments, through this committee, who have responsibility for arranging appropriate departmental training. The role of the committee is recognised as important in striking a balance between whole school training issues and departmental needs.

The increased funding for professional development, and the increased delegation to departments, has been met with universal appreciation from staff. As one member of the senior staff put it: 'The money spent on professional development is vital in these times of constant change.' Another felt that: 'Staff have welcomed the increased opportunities for professional development – their awareness of the existence of opportunities has certainly been heightened.' Many departments had used the funds to have whole team training, usually focusing on the National Curriculum, often held off-site. Having time to plan schemes of work was also seen as a very real benefit. The head of English sums up the opportunities staff are taking:

We have a departmental professional development budget to cover staff, courses and whole department training. There is a separate budget for special cases of professional career development – we can bid into this. In the department we surveyed all training on offer locally and tend to concentrate on in-house whole department training – most of the budget will be used for cover. Cascade doesn't work effectively – it doesn't have the same effect.

As the school had recently bought in the services of a neighbouring authority advisory service, departments were just beginning to make use of this expertise. Although it is early days in which to make any judgement on the impact of the new arrangements for professional development, the school is aware of the importance of staff training as a key factor in the effective use of other resources for supporting curriculum delivery.

Increased school autonomy through grant maintained status has increased the administrative and managerial workload within the school. In order to handle this with least disruption to existing staff, a school administrator has been appointed who also acts as clerk to the governing body. The impact of this new appointment was felt most by senior management, not only in the financial and management information readily made available on which to base decisions, but also in taking the administrative load from the Senior Management Team. Thus, the roles of the deputy head teachers have been redefined to allow them to focus on curriculum, staff development and pastoral matters respectively. While one deputy still retains a brief for building matters, day-to-day administration is now taken care of by the administrator. In this advisory capacity the administrator attends senior management and governing body meetings as necessary. While there may have been some initial hesitation on the part of existing staff regarding the new appointment, the present incumbent was undoubtedly providing an excellent service to the school. As one member of senior management explained: 'With GM this role is significant – I don't think we could have possibly introduced GM without such a position.' Both teaching and non-teaching staff were, to a lesser extent, beginning to welcome the support. Comments such as 'the administrator has been very beneficial to the non-teaching staff – we have a ready point of contact for queries and concerns' demonstrate the developing relationship. While some initial concerns had been expressed about the cost of the new appointment, and some staff were still not quite sure of what the role entailed, there was an acceptance of the support he provided for senior management. Those staff who had cause to deal with the administrator were quite clear, however, of the benefits of the much shorter chain of command in reporting and responding to minor repairs in the school. One head of department described this as having 'a major impact on my job'.

Other benefits of autonomy and grant maintained status include the ability to allocate resources for the attraction and retention of well-qualified and motivated teachers. Members of the governing body spoke of their desire to keep the morale of existing staff high and were aware of potential stress levels. Projects such as the staff marking area and the appointment of the administrator, it was hoped, would help to ensure this. Moreover, the average size of form groups was being 'kept down to reasonable proportions with an average of 25 pupils in a group' and plans for September 1993 were to create an extra class for new entrants. Staff were said to be 'overjoyed' at this prospect and the benefits of smaller pupil groups were also appreciated by parents. The importance of keeping pupil teaching groups small was endorsed by the 94 per cent of parents who agreed with the statement 'It is important to keep pupil teaching groups small'. It was recognised that these improvements were only possible as a result of an increased budget.

RESOURCE MANAGEMENT

In order to understand how the school allocates resources, and the extent to which decisions are informed by curriculum needs, it is necessary to look at the decision-making process. We begin by looking at the formal structures of decision making which have been put in place at Whittaker School, particularly in the light of grant maintained status, and then comment on how those structures are being interpreted in practice at the level of the whole school and in departments and faculties.

The structures of decision making

The head teacher of Whittaker School described the structure of decision making as one which 'revolves around a number of governors' committees each of which is chaired by a member of the governing body and school based committees chaired by members of senior management'.

The governing body has four executive committees which report back minutes of meetings to the main termly meeting, where decisions are ratified. These cover: curriculum, finance, personnel and marketing. One or more of the Senior Management Team attends each of these committees which are the main forums for resource management decisions. School-based committees are Senior Curriculum Committee (comprising heads of faculty and chaired by the curriculum deputy) and Senior Pastoral Committee (comprising heads of school and pastoral year tutors and chaired by the pastoral deputy). These committees meet once per half term. There is also a representative Staff Development Committee. There is no parallel representation of governors on school-based committees but a hybrid school-based committee for buildings is made up of both staff and governors and chaired by the deputy with responsibility for buildings and finance. While the school still formally holds heads of department meetings once per term this forum has largely been replaced by the Senior Curriculum Committee. Faculty teams hold formal meetings at least once every half term but many hold extra sessions and pastoral teams hold twice termly meetings for upper and lower school. Senior management meets weekly and invites other senior members of staff as appropriate. The whole staff meet at the beginning of each half term. The school has made use of *ad hoc* working groups in recent years, often linked to a particular policy initiative such as equal opportunities or assessment recording and reporting. These again have tended to be led by senior management with invited representation from faculties.

Such a structure provides opportunities for consultation and participation and clear lines of communication. The governing body committee structure is so comprised to include senior management and thus provides an efficient system for staff and governors to collaborate. In this way the Senior Management Team articulates the voice of staff in policy decisions and provides professional expertise input into resource management decisions which are taken by the governing body.

The Development Plan

The school has just begun a cycle of school development planning. Such systematic planning for school improvement is new at Whittaker School and the head teacher acknowledges that the first plan was derived primarily from her own priorities and perceptions of the school's strengths, weaknesses and future needs. Of significance to the management of education resources are the criteria for planning which particularly link future developments to resources:

The Development Plan should meet criteria of all good planning. In particular, it is necessary that governors, Head and staff;
... take into account constraints e.g. lack of experience in some areas and lack of resources
... accurately calculate the costs of change (the costs of time, INSET, equipment)

Indeed, in identifying how school management practice will change in response to a systematic approach to development planning, four aspects are highlighted:

... planning for specific, observable outcomes
... planning within time-scales
... carefully costing change
... making priorities

These four criteria underline the role of school development planning in making explicit the link between resource management and school improvement. When resources are limited decisions have to be made on a priority basis. The importance of departmental plans as an input to the process is recognised: 'The department development plans are the real key to delivering effective change' and a rolling programme of department reviews by senior management has been put in train.

The development cycle begins in the autumn term in preparing departmental and faculty plans for the following academic year, to be submitted in January. At the same time, whole school developments are being formulated by senior management with governors, using the committees and working parties where appropriate. All staff are invited to contribute with suggestions for whole school developments, prompted by agenda items at staff and faculty meetings. Whole school priorities are not seen by senior management as just within its brief. In January, senior management discuss departmental plans with each department, assess whole school issues and draft the School Development Plan. The overall financial implications of the plan are assessed in the light of the school budget which is being drafted at the same time. By the end of the spring term the School Development Plan and the budget have been approved by governors. Action plans from the Development Plan are drawn up during the summer term by senior management in consultation with faculties, detailing tasks, responsibilities and timescales, and a review is conducted to assess the present year's plans and inform future priorities.

The head teacher acknowledges that there was not a culture of consultation in the school prior to her arrival and while the school has always had an experienced and well-qualified staff, it was not part of the culture to encourage their ideas. Moreover, she recognises the potential threat to the secure environment in which staff have previously operated:

> It's very secure to have someone telling you what to do because if things go wrong you say 'well you told me to do that' . . . having now to think and make your own decisions and stick by them and see them through is a very insecure feeling.

The following sections will consider the management process within the school and within departments and the impact of both delegated decision making and school development planning.

Processes of whole school management

At Whittaker School, part of the role of senior management is to ensure a successful balance is achieved between the differentiated needs of departments and the needs of the school as a whole. The school development planning process is a key component for bringing this about and we draw upon the perceptions of staff and governors as well as evidence from our observation of committee meetings in order to help us understand how the process works. We also explore planning within the faculty structure in a later part of this section.

The role of the governing body

The qualities of members of the governing body at Whittaker School are a contributory factor to its approach to school governance. The school has a very supportive governing body composed of governors with much professional expertise. They have responded very positively to grant maintained status and welcome the increased funding and the freedom to manage their own affairs: 'The greatest improvement is that the school can set its own priorities and use its own assessments in allocating resources. There is now greater flexibility and fewer delays' (Vice Chair).

The governing body sees its role as policy maker. In this respect its involvement in decision making is limited to strategic issues. The Chair acknowledged: 'Governors must take a broader look . . . (at the management of the school)'. At present, the head teacher and senior management provide information and draft policy for the governing body and, while governors are content, in the main, to defer to the role of senior management, there is no sense of rubber stamping decisions with staff quite clearly accountable for their recommendations and their implementation of those decisions. However, a new parent governor recognised that grant maintained status enables more direct accountability between funding and resource allocation decisions, but admitted that he did not fully understand the difference between local management and grant maintained status. At those meetings we observed, governors displayed clear understanding of issues through their pertinent questions with the head teacher and staff providing full information on which decisions could be based. As one deputy observed: 'It would be very unlikely for the governing body or its finance committee to overturn any professional decisions – they are there as a check – an exercise in accountability.' Few formal links exist between governors and staff but, nevertheless, governors did appear to be aware of the curriculum needs of the school, understood the priorities which had to be made and emphasised the importance of the quality of staff and the conditions of working, which governors had been determined to improve following grant maintained status.

The views of parents in Table 7.5 endorse high satisfaction with the principle of a governing body: 95 per cent of parents agreed with the statement that 'Having a governing body is a good thing for the school'. Just over half of those replying to the survey agreed that they would like to have more of a say in what goes on in school and more of a say in how the school spends its money. While this does not represent a high level of dissatisfaction, it is not a complete statement of satisfaction. In the open comment section of our questionnaire, no parent referred to the responsibilities of the governing body when asked to comment on their impressions of grant maintained status.

Table 7.5 Year 9 parents: Whittaker School

What I think	strongly agree (%)	agree (%)	disagree (%)	strongly disagree (%)
Having a governing body is a good thing for the school	24.1	70.4	3.7	1.9
I would like more of a say in how the school spends its money	11.7	48.6	34.2	5.4
I would like to have more of a say in what goes on in school	6.1	47.4	43.9	2.6

The role of the head teacher and senior management

Since gaining grant maintained status the senior management has been restructured with the appointment of an administrator. His appointment has freed the deputies from some of their administrative tasks and given them time to become more closely involved in faculties. Now, the head teacher and the three deputies each have formal links with two faculties (one in which they teach and another in which they do not) and attend faculty meetings as observers. As a result of grant maintained status two of the three deputies have become budget holders, one for staff development and training and another for capital projects. Each chairs the appropriate school committees.

The role of the newly appointed head teacher in introducing new management processes into the school and managing the change to grant maintained status should not be underestimated. Her contribution is summed up by one member of staff: 'It would seem there is a happy marriage between grant maintained philosophies and those of the Head in terms of more efficient use of resources and greater involvement of staff in the development planning process.' The pivotal role of the head teacher is clear in the relationship between senior management and the governing body as she has made the deliberate – although not uncommon – decision to attend all governing body committees since the school became grant maintained.

Staff participation

There is a clear feeling that staff understand the role of senior management in establishing the development planning process. In a few cases, however, staff feel that such consultation as exists is tokenism and feel overlooked when they do not get feedback on the outcomes of decisions.

A member of the ancillary staff commented: 'I can only surmise that the head teacher and governors made the decisions that affect the school as a whole. I have no role in the decision making process within the school.' However, the majority of staff to whom we spoke understood the practical constraints of time attached to participation and consultation and were happy with the way in which the structure was operating in practice. As one member of staff told us: 'We are as well informed as practical – we are allowed to say what we think and are listened to – at any level – even if decisions are made elsewhere.'

There was no confusion about the change to development planning. A clear understanding of the link between identifying curriculum needs and linking these to resources was articulated:

The School Development Plan seems to me to drive the allocation of resources.

The School Development Plan is the basis for funding decisions.

Management of resources must be linked to development planning in a properly managed institution – which Whittaker is.

The role of the Staff Development Committee in particular provides a specific illustration of practice, highlighting positive relationships between senior management and staff and providing a good example of delegated resource management. The whole issue of staff training, according to one member of staff, has 'reinforced my sense of whole school needs'. While a Staff Development Committee existed prior to the school gaining grant maintained status, the allocation of a substantially increased budget for this activity from the DFEE has sharpened its focus. One deputy was given charge of this budget and is accountable for it. He works with the Development Committee, which has representation from pastoral staff and all faculties. Throughout the year, the committee provides a forum for consultation, feedback and up to date information on training opportunities, including the allocation of sessions bought in from the inspectorate of a neighbouring local authority.

Much of the discussion observed in this committee centred on practical, administrative issues, although concerns were also articulated. Representatives at the meeting were anxious to convey perceived training needs and offer suggestions for training delivery, in-house and by external agencies. As a result, many ideas and suggestions were generated from staff and the onus lay with the Chair effectively to include these in future programmes. Perceptions of the success of the committee would appear to rest with staff taking the view that future training did respond to their needs and that the committee Chair, as budget holder, not only had the authority to act but would do so.

The role of the administrator

The school administrator is a new appointment. Senior management and governors recognised the importance of efficient systems for management and the need for financial information to inform decision making. Not only does the administrator have responsibility for maintaining such systems, his opinion is also sought on future expenditure plans. In this way, as the head teacher acknowledged, he has quite an influential role. As clerk to the governing body he attends all governing body meetings, including committees, to provide information and advice in a way similar to that a local authority officer might provide for the governing body of a locally managed school. As a member of the school staff, however, his is a different perspective from that of such an officer.

As the administrator acknowledges, his post is an expense to the school and, as a result of grant maintained status, he provides some of the services which would previously have been provided by the local authority. However, he maintains that the advantages of the 'ownership and autonomy' thus generated within the institution, together with benefits for flexibility and speed of decision making, bring considerable benefits to the school. He regards the School Development Plan as vital: 'We are in a business situation – you can't run a £3m business on an *ad hoc* basis.' In common with the head teacher, he acknowledges that at present he has too much input into the development planning process and hopes that with time his role will diminish by comparison with contributions from staff. His assessment of the role of resource management in school improvement is cautious:

> Education resource management is only part of the picture. Some departments you could plough money into with no effect at all. Others could do much with a very small amount of money. It's the quality of the human resources which counts.

Processes of management in faculties and departments

The way in which faculties function and the role of the head of faculty are an essential element of how resource decisions can be translated into classroom practice. At Whittaker we interviewed staff members and observed faculty meetings in order to identify how this was happening.

Role of heads of faculty and department

Heads of faculty and heads of department at Whittaker are responding positively to responsibilities for delegated resource management. While the departmental budgets have been increased, some departments feel they may have lost out as allowances for practical subjects seem not to have been resolved to everyone's satisfaction. However, the response to development planning varies across departments with some adapting more vigorously to the new culture than others. One head of department expressed some frustration with feedback from senior management:

> Departments/faculties draw up their own development plans, identifying priorities and costing. These are submitted to SMT *but I* feel excluded from (a) how decisions are *then* made re. funding and (b) any response/feedback on my submission. I think this is seen as a weakness to be addressed. . . . I have some influence on decisions, particularly re. curriculum matters. The decision-making process re. funding/staffing is less 'open' – we submit development plans, costing, INSET plans, bids for special/extra funds, but the *decision-making* happens elsewhere.

Other departments identified the resources budget as crucial:

> The resources budget is crucial – crisis point. Previously we could reserve funds for special equipment, now the budget is not big enough. We put forward a development plan for substantial physics resources – this was picked up but not responded to – we are hopeful for next year. . . . I don't feel the school (development plan) priorities are identified by us. I'm not sure of the process – I don't feel I could recollect the School Development Plan and we are not reacting with our departmental plans – they should be on the wall. Planning has been difficult in times of immediate crisis. I don't feel I'm involved in whole school priorities.

While these illustrations cannot be said to be typical, they do express some of the frustrations that middle managers have about their role and, in particular, their position in understanding whole school needs in relation to those of their own faculty. If heads of faculty are developing a sense of whole school priorities it is likely to be through their participation in the Senior Curriculum Group. This is described by the Chair as a key group in school, 'an engine house'. In discussion on major curriculum issues this group will consider resource implications in open discussion. Heads of department are asked to consider the implications of decisions made with their department and report back to the group. In practice, however, from the meetings we observed of the group, staff still need to resolve fundamental curriculum policy issues before a real understanding of whole school priorities can develop. Indeed, there was much confusion about the process of curriculum audit and review – notably the extent to which governors should be involved – and some disagreement on curriculum philosophy. At all times, the head teacher actively encouraged staff to contribute to discussion in the Senior Curriculum Group, and emphasised the importance of reaching a consensus, but heads of department clearly have difficulties resolving the tension between their whole school responsibilities and departmental representation.

Not unexpectedly, heads of department found their intra-departmental role easier and the delegated professional development budget provides a good example. Faculty members clearly understand the system of delegation and welcome the opportunity to take more control over their training needs The head of geography sums this up: 'INSET is now devolved to departments – this is marvellous. I can train to meet the needs of the department – we took two days out for the whole department to look at assessment procedures and new schemes of work'.

The technology faculty provides another illustration of a new sense of empowerment. On training for Key Stage 3 schemes of work, the head of faculty explained: 'I shopped around for providers. The LEA was far too expensive. I used the cheapest. We had an excellent day.' He regards the extra administration as a price worth paying for his freedom to choose and is planning a similar training this year for Key Stage 4.

Staff as part of the departmental team

Our interview data suggest that teaching staff are also affected by a tension between their understanding of whole school perspectives and their role in decision making on these, as against decisions within their own departments. One member of staff commented: 'Within the department all needs are thrashed out in departmental meetings – it is a democratic department. At school level, I don't know how priorities are set.' In general, departmental priorities are being addressed with staff consultation and departments hold regular team meetings on administrative and curriculum issues.

One faculty provides an illustration of this in practice:

In the department when we look at the School Development Plan (and update it) we obviously put down our needs and priorities. We have regular and very good meetings in our faculty. . . . We are working on whole-school priorities but before the new head teacher came there simply didn't seem to be any! The school has been dragged forward into the 90s very quickly. There has been a tremendous amount of work done in the last three years but obviously the whole-school issues will continue to take time to establish themselves.

A recent agenda for the departmental meeting provides an illustration of key issues for discussion:

1. School Curriculum Policy Statement
2. Year 8 progress
3. Years 8 and 9 Record Booklets
4. Years 8–10 Tests
5. Updating/Revising Departmental Documents
6. A.O.B.

The majority of these items concern curriculum-related administrative issues and discussions were collaborative in nature. In this respect no business referred to specific resource management issues. Item 1 had been referred to faculties from the Senior Curriculum Group and a full discussion took place in the faculty on the possible aims of such a policy statement. All members of staff participated, although feedback tended to be negative rather than constructive. In the Senior Curriculum Group, the head teacher had emphasised the importance of the school formulating this key policy but its significance, in this respect, was not communicated so forcefully within the faculty.

Other departments believed they are being overlooked in resource allocation. Despite serving on the Buildings Committee, the head of home economics claimed she had failed to persuade senior management of the need to refurbish the home economics area, despite arguing on health and safety grounds. As action was only taken after a visit from an inspector this left the member of staff feeling inadequate to influence decisions. Similarly, the head of physics felt that the departmental budget was not adequate and pointed out that despite bidding for substantial funds in the departmental plan, these were not approved. Others acknowledged the task which a new administration had faced:

> The school has *so* much to do because of the previous administration, so I guess a lot of time and resources are being spent on making sure that it is at least up-to-date. I feel that the school is being managed very efficiently from the top so far as systems and premises are concerned but I would like to see a greater concentration on the human resources in the future and I'm sure this will happen. I will continue to make this point anyway!

CONCLUSION: CHALLENGING AND LEADING

Whittaker School has faced the challenge of adapting to local management and the greater autonomy of grant maintained status at the same time as adjusting to a new head teacher who has brought a different approach to school management. While her approach is fully supported by the senior management team and the governing body, it is a change with which some staff are still coming to terms. Moving from a more traditional approach to management and leadership is clearly challenging some of the staff who have to understand the different tensions involved in a headship role which offers leadership but also expects others to participate in decision making.

These changes are occurring in a school which already had recognised strengths so that the aim is to improve still further. The capacity of the new head teacher to lead that improvement is a view endorsed by many parents, Table 7.6 showing that 93 per cent agreed with the statement 'The school is well led by the head teacher'. The smooth working relationship which exists between senior management and the governors is one manifestation of this leadership. There is also a positive response among staff to the new leadership and the new status of the school but the changes have also brought a degree of uncertainty as staff adjust to the new expectations made of them. Some of these uncertainties are apparent when we assess how the school meets the characteristics we identify with cost-effectiveness.

Evidence of *radical audit* in Whittaker is apparent in the school's review of its premises. The alterations to the libraries, the introduction of a marking area for staff, changes to offices and toilets, carpeting of rooms, new furniture and blinds are examples of actual change. Plans for cloakrooms, accommodation for vocational business studies courses and curriculum suites for departments are included in a five-year rolling programme. The capital programme is providing a technology block and other bids are planned. These changes and plans illustrate the opportunity provided by LMS and GMS to review the use of premises and to act upon the review. Taken as a set, they are good examples of ways in which these opportunities can lead to a review and action in areas where change had been difficult. Our account also shows developments in funding profes-sional development and in the appointment of a school administrator where decisions have differed from the past and, in some degree, reflects a readiness to audit the existing use of staff and make changes. The scope for further opportunities to use (additional) resources more flexibly is recognised:

At a time when other schools in [the county] appear to be suffering from increasing difficulty in meeting their statutory duties on the budgets made available, Whittaker appears to have been able to use the funds granted to it in a more efficient manner and to allow staff and pupils to benefit from the more flexible use of allowances. The improvements to the school are noticeable, if long overdue.

Accounts of the role of the school administrator show school management as being informed by the *costs* of alternatives. Discussions at the governing body showed governors asking pertinent questions about proposals and receiving quite full information from senior staff on the financial implica-tions of proposals. As with Broome and Skelton, there was no evidence of departmental costs being itemised other than those associated with learning materials and professional development.

There is clear evidence of *internal delegation* of responsibility over some resources. Funds for learning materials have been substantially increased, by 30 per cent on the change to local management and doubled with the grant maintained status. Responsibility for this spending rests with departments. Significant expenditure on professional development has also been delegated with departments shaping their own priorities in consultation with the Staff Development Committee.

The role of the Staff Development Committee is a good example of a *dialogue of accountability* at the school. It has the responsibility of managing the legitimate professional development needs of departments with those for the school as a whole. Ensuring that appropriate needs are met must require discussions whereby those involved satisfy themselves that resources are being matched to needs. This dialogue also occurs through the preparation of the Development Plan. The process begins in the autumn as departments prepare their plans and senior management considers whole school issues. These come together in January as the financial implications of proposals need to be costed. This process and the supporting structure is in its infancy at Whittaker and it is apparent that there are tensions. In particular, some staff were not convinced that the process of participation was a genuine attempt to involve them in the process of decision making. The majority of staff, on the other hand, appeared to recognise practical constraints to some forms of participation and took a positive view of the change:

> Very early days yet. Both governors and head seem to be forward looking and aware of the responsibilities they now have. Everyone is still involved in a learning curve about GM so mistakes are made and toes trodden on, but the general impression is that we are doing reasonably well.

It may be that some of the uncertainties about the new approach to management are a consequence of two forms of unease. One arises from concern about new roles expected of heads of department and members of staff from a head teacher who is challenging them to be more actively involved in decisions than had been the case under the previous Head. A second and closely related unease may reflect uncertainty as to how staff assess the balance to be struck between *challenging* and *leading*. There is little doubt that the head teacher has her own views about the need for change and head teacher and staff will have to learn to live with the tensions inherent in the practice arising from applying these two concepts. The dialogue of accountability was also apparent at meetings of the governors. While policy proposals were not rejected, we were aware that discussions of the governing body had no sense of decisions simply being 'rubber-stamped' and were occasions for active questioning of proposals.

Our survey data show a high degree of satisfaction with the head teacher and, in some respects, this is *prima facie* evidence that decisions made by school management are matched to priorities as seen by others. In these respects, there is no evidence of the *detachment of management*. Evidence of team meetings, as well as the role of appraisal, point to the role of a professional dialogue in informing management and limiting its detachment. Whether the processes in place are sufficient is a theme to which we will return together with a discussion of access to sources of information which are *independent* of the staff.

In all of this, the distinctive impact of grant maintained status is not easy to distinguish. There are clearly welcome changes in the level of resources to the school, a benefit illustrated by the comment of one Year 9 pupil:

> I enjoy Whittaker and have settled in nicely. I think the improvements to the school are brilliant and looking forward to finding out what other improvements are going to take place.

A comment from one parent, however, showed more caution:

> My own positive opinion is that the process of going grant maintained has not yet produced any noticeable improvements in staff/budget and staff/parent relations. These relations were not particularly bad before – they are just not any better.

The circumspection about resources is echoed in the response (Table 7.6) of Year 9 parents, 58 per cent of whom disagreed with the statement 'The school seems to have a lot of money'. It may be that the financial benefits of grant maintained status are not yet apparent to many parents, as well as some staff and pupils. It may also be that high expectations of what might be achieved detract from what has so far been possible.

The importance for school improvement of the greater resource delegation contained within the grant maintained initiative is recognised by the school administrator who acknowledges that plans for the future will rest on directing resources to improve standards:

> The whole aim of GM is to allow greater flexibility of control and endeavour to improve the educational standards of pupils who pass through the school. Hopefully we are directing the resources into areas which we feel will lead to improved standards of teaching (through progressive development), smaller class sizes (through improved staffing ratios), a more pleasant learning and teaching environment (through

Table 7.6 Year 9 parents: Whittaker School

What I think	strongly agree (%)	agree (%)	disagree (%)	strongly disagree (%)
The school is well led by the head teacher	29.7	63.1	5.4	1.8
The school seems to have a lot of money	4.0	39.6	46.5	9.9

building refurbishment) and a wider variety of teaching materials available (through increased capitation).

This is a comment which recognises the principal empirical test of the delegation of management responsibility over resources. Is delegation leading to school improvement and, in addition, does the degree of delegation matter? If delegation of resource management is a component of school improvement and a means for schools to be more cost-effective, a key empirical question concerns the degree of delegation which is optimal. Is the level of delegation represented by LMS likely to be more or less cost-effective than GMS or is the optimum some other mix of delegated responsibilities?

Part III

Securing improvement

Chapter 8

Assessing improvement

We began this enquiry into good practice in education resource management with the intention of examining three questions:

- How are these secondary schools using their greater responsibilities over educational resources?
- What are the characteristics of the decision-making processes which relate resources to learning?
- How is the exercise of these responsibilities linked to the standard and quality of learning in the schools?

In this chapter, our purpose is to draw upon the information collected from the 18 schools to provide a summary conclusion to those questions. We begin with a *descriptive* section which shows the diversity of ways in which these schools have actually used their new responsibilities. While these are all cases identified at greater length in the previous four chapters, our summary shows clearly the breadth of opportunities and actions taken as a result of the local management and grant maintained initiatives. This is followed by a section *analysing* how the effects on learning are assessed and we examine the language used by our interviewees to describe the contribution of specific resource decisions to the processes of teaching and learning in their school. We believe this material not only gives us some insights into how resource decisions are assessed in schools but has implications for how schools might improve their management of resources. In the third section we consider the decision-making arrangements in the schools we visited. These are interpreted and *explained* in the context both of the section on how the effects on learning are assessed and our own argument about the characteristics of a cost-effective school. The whole provides a basis for the final chapter in which we consider the implications of our study for the management of schools and for the policy context in which they are located.

USING DELEGATION

The 18 secondary schools we visited have welcomed and used the delegation of powers contained in LMS and GMS. Chapters 4, 5, 6 and 7 are evidence of the range of activities at which resources have been directed. In this summary we give an example of one school where the case cited has occurred but this does not mean that the event has only happened once. Our reference allows the reader to refer to that case in the relevant chapter. We include examples of some initiatives which could have been introduced without powers arising from LMS and GMS, and we do so because they were viewed by those whom we interviewed as cases which arose from delegation. In the sense that delegation may be changing the *perception* of school managers as to what is possible, we believe it is legitimate to give these as examples of change arising from delegation. That delegation may be changing the culture in schools as to what is possible is a theme to which we return in Chapter 9.

Teaching staff

Many of those interviewed described how delegation had allowed them to make staffing decisions which matched their needs. It has meant:

- employing more teachers (School 6);
- using the curriculum analysis to determine the complement of teachers (Skelton);
- the casual employment of teachers for covering absent teachers is used less (School 8);
- reductions in class size (School 3);
- being able to plan ahead and protect key areas of the curriculum at a time when pupil numbers in a school suffered a temporary fall (School 10);
- employing additional teachers for the development of Information Technology across the curriculum (School 13);
- appointing an outreach teacher (School 1).

Delegation has given schools greater flexibility:

- replacing a departing deputy with a senior teacher (School 3);
- the responsibilities of senior staff have been reviewed and altered (School 18);
- funding has allowed for more non-teaching time for heads of department (School 6);
- more time has been purchased to provide more tutorial time (School 7);
- more imaginative deployment of staff in schools with community education provision (School 12);
- earmarking time for curriculum co-ordination and advising departments of the production of learning materials (School 14);

- the ability to advertise and make new appointments more quickly (School 13).

Delegated responsibility over pay, conditions and professional development have been put to use:

- Incentive Allowances have been used to support specific new developments (School 6);
- significant increases in the numbers of staff on Incentive Allowances (School 14);
- moving time-limited Incentive Allowances between departments to implement an Information Technology policy across the school over a period of years;
- increasing the earmarked budget for professional development (School 10);
- delegating the professional development to departments (School 16).

Support staff for the curriculum

Schools are rethinking their use of support staff in terms of the direct assistance they can offer the curriculum. There are several examples of librarians being appointed and increases in many categories of support staff. These appointments show schools exercising their judgement about the appropriate mix of staff skills and are a departure from earlier practice in schools in England and Wales. As with a study of the innovative uses of non-teaching staff in schools (Mortimore and Mortimore with Thomas, 1994), our study includes examples which have parallels with that enquiry. As with that study, these 18 schools judge that appointing staff with the appropriate blend of skills satisfies the principle of fitness-for-purpose:

- appointments of qualified librarians and assistants working with students on project work (School 12);
- specialist in Information Technology working with students (Skelton);
- additional technicians in Science who facilitate more practical work (School 6);
- reprographics technicians who can transform the presentation and speed of production of in-house learning materials;
- classroom support workers in Mathematics (School 3);
- clerical assistance for the preparation of learning materials (School 5).

Administration

Delegation has increased the administrative demands on schools. In responding to these demands, many of the schools have used delegation to review their systems of administration so that resources are being matched to needs. Non-teaching staff are emerging in important roles and, in the case study schools, Skelton has reduced its complement of deputy head teachers and Whittaker has appointed an administrator to a senior position in the management structure:

- using computerised information systems to handle pupil records and reporting (School 4);
- using computerised information systems to produce a personal examination timetable and seating plan for each student (School 3);
- creation of new administrative posts to respond to specialised demands (School 8).

An environment for learning

All 18 schools have used delegation to alter and improve the fabric of the building and enhance facilities for staff and students. The opportunity to make improvements to the premises has clearly been welcomed and used creatively. It is an area where delegation appears to have stimulated an audit of the use of premises and many new initiatives:

- reorganising the whole school so that, over time, the accommodation is adapted into curriculum area suites (School 6);
- reorganising specific departments where curriculum suites are seen as a priority (School 8);
- redecoration and refurbishment of classrooms (School 10);
- improvement to the school environment, inside and outside the classroom, over a five-year period (School 9);
- altering accommodation to provide a curriculum area for Information Technology (School 3);
- altering accommodation to place clusters of computers in departments (School 16);
- redesigning space to create a *model office* for business studies (School 17);
- altering accommodation to improve library facilities (School 8).

Curriculum materials

Funding for learning materials appears to have been increased in these schools, using a variety of means to allocate the money:

- changes in the way money allocated with greater use of formula-based systems (School 17);
- open debate is also used to allow departments to understand the rationale for allocations to departments (School 14);
- money is earmarked for new developments (School 7);

- substantial additional funds to support the work of a new head of department (School 9);
- expenditure on reprographic support to improve in-house learning materials (School 5);
- funding the release of staff time to work on curriculum projects (School 7).

External relations and support

The autonomy represented by delegation has made schools more aware of the importance of undertaking initiatives with external groups and agencies which can support the work of the school. Some of these initiatives could and did occur before LMS and GMS. We draw attention to such developments for two reasons. Some are mentioned because they involve changes which link the delegated budget to other funds; others because the search for and use of external support appears to be a consequence of changing attitudes to resource management in schools. It may also be that changes in the membership of governing bodies as a result of the 1986 Education Act, notably the growth of representation from business and commerce, is giving added emphasis to this development.

Support from the local community:

- linking PTA funds to the delegated budget to improve library facilities (School 5);
- finance, materials and expertise from members of the governing body (School 1);
- use of the premises to generate conference income (School 4);
- use of a community facility for the provision in the school (School 10);
- purchase of services – cleaning, grounds maintenance – at competitive rates.

Support from industry and commerce:

- computer equipment and accommodation provided by local business (School 6);
- greater use of student–industry links (School 5);
- use of local industry for staff training.

Support from training providers:

- use of University Project to support assessment in Mathematics (School 14);
- training staff using Training and Enterprise Councils (School 9).

Support from central and local government:

- grants for developing technology (School 8);

- joint expenditure to improve facilities which are used by school and community (School 12);
- more rigorous and planned use of an LEA's advisory service for professional development (School 14).

The examples provided in this section fall into two main categories. Many are cases of initiatives which were not available to schools before the introduction of LMS and GMS. In that respect they can clearly be identified as arising from the delegation of resource management. A second category consists of examples of changes which could have occurred before the introduction of these schemes of delegation. What appears to be occurring, however, is that delegation is altering perceptions of what is possible; some staff in some of the schools are now *seeing* development opportunities for the first time. Even if this change in perception is leading to developments which could have happened before, we suggest they can be attributed to the change in context brought about by LMS and GMS.

These examples of the use of delegation tell us a good deal about how schools have taken the opportunities provided by LMS and GMS. Many changes are being introduced which would not have occurred without delegation and show *prima facie* evidence of schools auditing their deployment of resources and making changes as a result of that. These changes alone, however, tell us comparatively little about their consequence for the standard and quality of learning. An important component of all our interviews and surveys, therefore, involved asking people to assess the impact on the learning of pupils and students of the changes they cited. We draw upon responses to these questions in the next section.

ASSESSING THE EFFECTS ON LEARNING

Individuals and groups tend to evaluate the effects of LMS and GMS in different ways. When asked how the changes affected teaching and learning, for example, we would expect the perception and judgement of teachers to differ from that of members of the governing body. For that reason we report assessments of the effect of LMS and GMS in sections which represent the different groups involved. Such an approach assists in illuminating patterns in responses from these groups and acts as a guide to understanding what is taking place and inform future development. As in the previous section, we cite comments which illustrate the responses in our interviews and surveys, and readers should recognise that we could have included other similar examples.

School governors

Members of the governing body have the statutory responsibility for resource management in these schools. How do they assess the impact of delegation on the core activity of the school as a centre of teaching and learning?

- a major professional development project meant teachers were learning more of the methodologies of learning (School 16);
- additional clerical support has freed the Head's time (School 8);
- more money means less sharing of books and better learning materials (School 15);
- control of the premises as a GM school means community access can be increased (School 16);
- the school has become more focused upon its role as a caring environment (Broome);
- teaching loads have been re-arranged (Skelton);
- IT is an area of weakness which requires more resources (Skelton);
- more able students can now be taught in "express" groups (Skelton);
- improvements to morale (Whittaker);
- more needs to be done to purchase equipment as money becomes available (Whittaker);
- class sizes have been kept down (Whittaker).

As might be expected, governors often cite the benefits in terms of tangible changes in resources rather than in observable changes in the day-to-day experience of students in classrooms. This is not always the case, however, some of the comments reporting on changes in teaching methodologies or changes in ethos, such as the idea of a 'caring environment'. Expressing the benefits of resource decisions in terms of the resources themselves is an understandable response by governors, many of whom will have limited confidence, ability and information to express outcomes in terms of changes in teaching and learning. Is this a satisfactory state of affairs, however, and as much as might reasonably be expected of members of governing bodies? Ought we, instead, to expect governors to have a language of improvement which is closer to the core activities of teaching and learning? In terms of their statutory duties, which require resources to be managed to meet curriculum obligations, this would be a reasonable expectation. Whether or not it is realistic depends upon how governors engage in what we have called the dialogue of accountability and is an issue we will examine in the final main section of this chapter. For the present, we must recognise that the language of improvement used by governors is often a language of resources and processes rather than a language of teaching or learning.

Senior staff

Governors were not alone in finding difficulty in assessing the impact of delegation on teaching and learning. While head teachers, senior staff and other teachers were more able to provide accounts in these terms, they also had difficulty. We begin with comments made by head teachers and senior staff:

- teachers in a better psychological frame of mind when in front of the class (School 3);
- the majority of girls get the subjects they choose which leads to better staff/student relations (School 13);
- teachers feel better equipped to deal with the National Curriculum (School 16);
- technician support means smooth running of the lab. and greater use of video equipment (School 1);
- rapid response in producing high quality learning materials (School 5);
- improved environment has made a difference to the ethos of the school (School 9);
- learning centre has assisted students to take more responsibility for their own learning (School 3);
- the bottom line is to motivate staff (School 6).

In some ways these comments bear comparison with those of governors. Often the benefit is expressed in some tangible way, such as the production of high quality learning materials. Benefit is also expressed as an indirect expression of impact on the learning experiences of pupils, as in the references to the capacities, competencies and motivation of teaching staff. As with governors, the language of senior staff in responding to our questions on the effect of resource decisions is often a language of resources and processes. That this should be so raises concerns about the basis upon which senior managers are assessing the effects of resource choices. If it reflects the detachment of management from the core activity of schools it has implications for the quality of their resource decisions. It may be, however, that the design of our enquiry is responsible for these replies, and researchers must always consider whether and how the design of their enquiry shapes the information they obtain. In effect, are our answers an artefact of our mode of enquiry?

In this respect, the first question we put to those whom we interviewed concerned resource choices. In the first phase of our enquiry, this led to the question 'What contribution has this change made to the processes of teaching and learning in the school?' During the case studies, the comparable question asked for their assessment of the resource choice in terms of 'effect on teaching and learning; have they improved the school; what effect have they had on pupils?' Might it be that by focusing upon resource choices at the beginning of an interview, answers to subsequent questions remained within a resource framework. We cannot know for sure whether this is the case or whether a language of resource and process does indeed represent the way senior staff actually assess the effects of their resource decisions. Our contention, however, is that these replies do properly reflect the language of senior staff and we suggest this for three reasons.

First, having received a resource or process reply, we sometimes asked a supplementary question to press them on the "effect on pupils", although this rarely led to a different answer. Second, these answers bear comparison with findings by HMI which report on the weakness of monitoring systems in schools. In effect, management is detached from the core activities of teaching and learning and, therefore, not as informed about them as it might be. It is not surprising, therefore, if the language of senior managers on the impact of resource decisions is more a language of resources and less a language of classroom change. There is also some consistency between these replies and findings of the 'Impact' Project (Bullock and Thomas, 1994) which noted the correlation of views on the positive effects on learning of local management with evidence of increases in resources. Third, our line of questioning did not always lead to the same result. When we review the comments of teachers, there is a difference in the language used and they are much closer to describing changes in classroom activity.

Teachers

It should not be surprising that teachers are best at giving accounts of effects which are close to the practice of the classroom, such as pupils receiving qualified help to do research assignments or classroom assistants working with the less able and more able, supporting better differentiation. These are important views and their classroom focus is a strong argument for senior management ensuring that the views of teachers are given due weight in the decision-making process:

- more effective mixed ability teaching (School 4);
- continuity and support to examination classes at a crucial time in the school year (School 13);
- children now do research assignments with qualified help – this provides equality of opportunity for children, not just those whose parents can help outside school (School 8);
- reprographics support makes it easier to set homework; no need for extensive notes (School 8);
- technician support to develop more practical work in Science (School 6);
- classroom support is enabling weaker groups to progress at a greater rate by giving each pupil more support (School 3);
- support assistants helping less able and more able; better differentiation (School 4);
- no deadlines for spending money; we can choose the best materials from publishers (School 8);

- word processing extends options for teaching and learning styles (School 16);
- with a drama studio, the quality of drama is improving and the motivation and attitude of pupils (School 6);
- professional development project has had a drastic change on the way maths is taught (School 14);
- library support staff has given pupils the incentive to do research and project work (Broome);
- no bottle-neck in reprographics which led to hasty, second rate lessons (Skelton);
- carpets in teaching rooms have improved the working environment, quieter, more civilised (Whittaker).

Support staff, parents, pupils and students

Direct quotes from support staff, parents, pupils and students are fewer and, with the exception of the support staff, limited to the three case study schools. In the case of parents, pupils and students our only source was the additional written comments returned with the questionnaire survey and only from the case study schools. Comments by support staff tend to emphasise provision, although there are references to process changes:

- delegation has brought about positive enhancement (Broome);
- support for staff provided by a technician and classroom support has led to more use of IT facilities by students (Skelton);
- money is spent – on learning materials – more effectively as a result of GM (Whittaker).

In the case of parents, it may be that their more general observations convey important messages about the importance of school ethos. They provide an alternative perspective which can deepen our understanding of their concerns about the schools which their children attend:

- The time my child has spent at Skelton has been a very happy time (Skelton);
- a distinct improvement in the amount spent on infrastructure (Whittaker);
- no noticeable improvements in staff/budget and staff/parent relations . . . not bad before – they are just not any better (Whittaker).

It is students who experience classroom practice directly and for whom it is a daily event. Their responses to our attitude survey and their additional written comments show them making sensible and realistic assessments of these experiences. Through surveys, school management could obtain regular feedback on the range of provision in the school:

- improving all the time in technology and learning (Broome);
- The school is brilliant. The teachers are nice and help you a lot. The school is clean and tidy and sets a high standard. Most topics are interesting or sometimes the teachers make it interesting. The school is excellent (Skelton).
- I enjoy Whittaker and have settled in nicely. I think the improvements to the school are brilliant and looking forward to finding out what other improvements are going to take place (Whittaker).

These comments convey a fundamental message with which we wholly concur, that resources are only part of much wider aspects of quality in schools. The management of decisions on resources is also part of the wider context of school management as a whole.

MANAGING THE PROCESS

In summarising our understanding of the decision processes which link resources to learning, our analysis is much influenced by the case studies of Broome, Skelton and Whittaker. In the 15 schools which we visited for one day, it was possible to collect a substantial amount of data on the range and kinds of resource choices made in these schools. Descriptions of decision-making processes, however, are less easily established in that time, not least because of the importance of obtaining multiple perspectives. This is not to say that we were not able to establish any view of these processes, rather that our data on the three case study schools are more extensive and have a bigger impact on our analysis.

We have organised our account, drawn from the data in Chapters 4, 5, 6 and 7, into two main parts. The first is organised around processes and areas of decision making and, *inter alia*, we consider relevant characteristics of the cost-effective school. In the second part, we discuss the people and groups that make these processes work and here also we consider the characteristics we would expect to see in cost-effective schools.

Decision making as a process

The schools we have studied exhibit a sense of purposeful leadership in their management of resources:

- there was little difficulty in identifying decisions on resources which were consistent with a wider and coherent framework of aims and priorities for the school (School 12).

In the first section of this chapter we cited many of the examples of how schools have used their responsibilities as locally managed and grant maintained schools. In some degree, these are evidence of *radical audit* with decisions on the allocation of resources reflecting fitness-for-purpose and creative use of the opportunities open to them. It is also apparent, above all in our more detailed enquiry in the case study schools, that these resource decisions were consistent with overall strategy in the schools.

Processes of development planning, as well as the content of the plan itself, showed the schools giving attention to *costs*. Typically, information on costs were reported using traditional line-budgets and none of the case study schools had their financial information cost-centred, apart from expenditure on learning materials and professional development. This does not mean that the schools did not have management information on resource allocations to subjects and departments because staffing informa-tion was available in the form of curriculum analyses. Whether it is appropriate for schools to move towards a more cost-centred financial information system is an issue we will consider in the final chapter.

Development planning was also used as a means for encouraging a *dialogue of accountability* with the staff, an important issue in overcoming the detachment of management. In the previous section, we noted that it is teaching staff who were most likely to use a language of teaching and learning to describe the effects of resource decisions and, therefore, their voice should be an important one in assessing needs:

- can provide the framework for linking resources to educational needs; a working document (School 6);
- can include statements of intent which do not make the distribution of the budget explicit in terms of money (Skelton);
- was a vehicle for wider staff participation (Skelton);
- is a means for creating a culture of participation (Whittaker);
- enables departmental plans to be linked to the school plan (Whittaker).

There was a demarcation with respect to those resources where decisions lay with departments and those which were for the school as a whole. Within departments there was clear evidence of participation in deciding spending priorities:

- regular departmental meetings are forums for all staff to participate in discussions on resource choices related to learning materials (Broome);
- departments can identify their needs and these are linked to the Faculty and School Plans (Skelton).

The type, purpose and significance of the resource, however, had a bearing upon the process of decision making:

- staff numbers and replacements were typically an area where decisions were made by the Head and Senior Management Team;
- marginal changes in staff numbers could include the head of the relevant department;

- decisions on administrative staff were the domain of Head and SMT;
- wider teaching staff involvement in decisions on the school environment;
- managing the school environment was normally a responsibility of senior staff;
- teaching staff decide on the purchase of learning materials;
- involving external support depends upon the nature of the external agency.

The examples and cases set out above show an *internal delegation* of responsibilities for some resources. The practice of having domains of decision may partly be influenced by the need to ensure that teaching staff concentrate on teaching and learning, senior management having a role in filtering those decisions which do not require a wider participation (Broome). While there are clear advantages of procedural efficiency in such a division, striking the right balance between participation and the time pressures associated with consultation is a challenge to head teachers and senior management who are powerful in regulating access to information and decision making. It is a judgement which affects the quality of the *dialogue of accountability* between interested groups in schools and these relationships are considered in the next part of the chapter.

Governors, head teachers and staff

A feature of the interview data from almost all the schools is that, while senior staff refer a good deal to the role of governors in decision making, this is in marked contrast to other members of the teaching staff who seldom mention governors. Equally, there is a set of committees to which teachers and senior staff refer but which is not mentioned by governors. It is a circumstance which illuminates the key role of the head teacher and senior staff in the decision making in the school. They are part of a dialogue of accountability with governors and part of a largely separate dialogue with staff. We argued in Chapter 3 that the quality of these dialogues is an important organisational attribute of the cost-effective school.

The quality of the dialogue with governors is a particularly important aspect of the wider accountability of education professionals to a wider public. The analysis of the data from the case studies suggests a number of features which relate to all three schools:

- members of governing bodies are becoming more knowledgeable about their role, committee work contributing to that change;
- governors see themselves as having a strategic role and are not rubber stamps, although head teachers expect to be advisers whose views are normally taken;

- governors also see themselves as being able to contribute individual skills and expertise as appropriate.

Earlier in this chapter, however, we drew attention to the language of improvement used by governors in assessing the effects of resource decisions and asked whether this language – dominated by comments on changes in resources – showed adequate knowledge of the core activity of schools for them to make informed judgements, even after receiving advice from senior staff. Our interview data and information from attendance at meetings indicate a significant variety in the quality of the dialogue of accountability between governors and senior staff.

There is clear evidence of accountability by listening, where governors listen to the reports which head teachers and teachers give them but ask few questions. While this is a limited form of accountability we should not understate the effect of an obligation to report since it requires the head teacher and teachers carefully to review the issues to be presented and consider what needs to be done. Second, there is accountability by questioning where governors draw upon their knowledge and expertise from other contexts to ask questions which explore the rationale of recommendations made by the head teacher or other staff. The test in this process is whether governors are satisfied by the quality of the answers they hear. A weakness of this dialogue, as with the first form of accountability, is the lack of *independent* information, recommendations being based largely on information provided by the head teacher and staff. That this should be so may all be very well in these schools but it would not be so if the person making the recommendations was part of the problem. In such circumstances, these forms of dialogue could lead governors to accept recommendations for new developments without having an adequate understanding of the underlying issues which the resource decisions are meant to tackle.

A third form of accountability is where governors and staff engage in a dialogue over information about the school which both groups have brought to the discussion. Visits to schools by governors can give rise to questions, and parent governors are another source of information which is independent of the staff. Over time, discussion in committees can also contribute to the quality of this form of accountability because governors will have encountered similar issues in the past. Through this process, a shared understanding of resource needs may emerge and can be the basis for governors making better informed decisions, although it will still fall short of information on teaching and learning – the core activity. What is clear in our case study schools is that governors are, to some extent, engaged in this form of dialogue with the head teacher and senior staff and, thereby, contribute to the quality of the resource judgements which are made.

A fourth form of accountability occurs where information is discussed which belongs neither to governors nor head teachers and is focused upon teaching and learning. Examinations results are one form of *independent* data which can be used to explore issues of teaching and learning and we visited schools where these were the basis of full discussions between the head teacher and governing body. Inspection reports provide another source, although none of the schools we attended were at a stage where an inspection report was current and, in any event, they will always be infrequent events in a school's history. Typically, therefore, governors appear to get little data about the core activities of teaching and learning which are independent of the head teacher and teachers. Whether this is a matter of concern will depend upon the quality of the advice given to governors by the head teacher and other staff and, in our case study schools, there was clear evidence of head teachers supporting the development of their governors as 'critical friends'. These circumstances cannot always be relied upon, however, and what should be done in those cases is a matter we consider in the final chapter.

Our earlier account and the information cited in the previous part of this chapter also shows that the head teacher and senior staff are also engaged in a dialogue with members of the teaching staff. This is clearly important as a means of overcoming the detachment of management but it is also valuable that the head teachers in Broome and Skelton examine the work of pupils, thereby providing themselves with an *independent* source of information on the quality of learning in the school. It is an important difference with governors who have relatively limited independent information. That the head teachers are in this position only serves to emphasise their pivotal role which, in all three schools, is interpreted differently, each giving shape and direction in distinctive ways:

- At Broome, staff had to be developed so that they had the confidence to contribute to policy debates about the development of the school. The head teacher believes that her staff have 'come on leaps and bounds . . . confident individuals who are far more ready to do things now than they would have been three or four years ago'. The need for more staff to be able to initiate and give leadership remains an issue, however, with too much dependent upon herself and her deputies.
- At Skelton, the head teacher acts as an *initiator* of many policies but he also acts as the *supporter* or sponsor of proposals made by others. This approach reflects conditions in the school which were aptly summarised in a comment by one teacher who suggested that Skelton is a school where there is, at present, an effective balance between leadership and active participation: 'I feel all Skelton staff are very professional and we are encouraged by SMT to take part in the planning of the school's requirements'.
- At Whittaker, the new head teacher must challenge a secure en-

vironment where teachers were accustomed to being told what to do and did not have to take the risk of making decisions. Her view is that she must challenge this environment where staff expect to be told what to do. It is a process upon which she has begun and which is seen as necessary, in order to create a culture which encourages people to have ideas and to express them.

In all three schools, the Senior Management Team plays an important role in working with and supporting the approach to leadership provided by the head teacher. The three schools also share a language of participatory management although, in each case, it is within the context of clear direction from the head teacher. Differences in the management of participation may reflect the different stages of development for each school, the level being appropriate for each school and its specific circumstances, and the judgement about this level of participation being made by each head teacher. It is an analysis of school management which is in danger of degenerating into an argument that 'good schools have good head teachers' and 'good head teachers' know how to judge particular needs in specific contexts. This is a conclusion we reject. We recognise that good head teachers may be a sufficient condition for creating a good school and that the case study schools did have good head teachers. We do not conclude from this, however, that good head teachers are a wholly necessary condition for schools becoming more cost-effective. Since not all schools can have good head teachers, such a conclusion would be tantamount to accepting that many schools are doomed to under-achieve. Our criteria for cost-effective schools are designed, therefore, for conditions where schools and the school system do not have to be entirely dependent upon the quality of one person in a single role. This is one of the themes we examine in the final chapter when we consider the implications of our study for the internal management of schools and the creation of an appropriate policy framework for ensuring that more schools can aspire to become more cost-effective in their performance. Such a discussion necessarily has implications for grant maintained schools and their potential as cost-effective institutions.

The impact of grant maintained status

That a grant maintained school receives more money than a locally managed school is, of itself, of limited significance in assessing the impact of the difference. It is the case, after all, that a GM school is responsible for paying for more services than an LM school. What is of greater significance is whether the additional funding is used more effectively and, further-more, whether the principle of extended autonomy has an additional effect on the culture of a GM school. In making these comments, we would stress that we visited only five GM schools and that a wider body of data from other studies is relevant to an assessment of these issues of effective resource management and the culture of autonomy.

The ability of GM schools to spend their additional funding to good effect is borne out by comments in Chapters 4 and 7:

- access to more resources increases morale, a sense of well-being and allows more needs to be met (Whittaker);
- more money provides greater scope for meeting needs (School 13).

The change also allows for greater flexibility in seeking suppliers for services and to pursue new initiatives:

- the ability to develop and change at speed (School 9);
- greater flexibility to improve educational standards (Whittaker).

This ability to develop and respond carries within it the possibility that the greater autonomy of GM status may be a distinctive attribute which is different from the initial awareness of autonomy and choice which must come from receiving a larger budget. Whether it is more than that initial awareness is an aspect which is of potentially great significance. In terms of differences in resource management, our summary indicates that the GM schools were using their additional funding to good effect and that there was an appreciation of the greater flexibility. What is not clear is whether the greater autonomy of GM schools is itself an important and distinguishing attribute enhancing, for example, the whole ethos of the school and long term commitment of the staff. We are not able to make such an assessment, not least because of the numbers of schools involved. For the future, student and parent responses in LM and GM schools may well provide comparative data on how or whether the autonomy of GM schools impacts on student experiences of learning. In the meantime, however, we do have a general concern about the nature of delegation in England and Wales and whether the structure is over-reliant on having head teachers like many of those whom we met in this study. Our final chapter explores this and other matters.

CONCLUSION: MANAGING IMPROVEMENT

There is no doubt that the 18 schools visited in the course of this study were using their delegated powers creatively. We not only have cited a wide range of developments arising directly from these new responsibilities but give examples of changes in relations with external bodies which appear to be a consequence of their greater autonomy. As much might be expected, however, from a set of schools selected because they were judged to be exemplars of good practice in the management of resources. More demanding conditions must be met if they are also to be

viewed as cost-effective schools. This requires us, first, to make judgements about the impact of resource choices on learning and, second,
whether organisational characteristics are in place to sustain the schools
as cost-effective institutions.

Resource choices and learning

Evidence about the impact of resource choices on learning comes from the
interviews and surveys. Our focus in these was on assessments of quality
as against the measurement of standards. This is partly because the scale
and design of the project would not have allowed for such measurement
but, more important, we would not expect to separate *measured* changes
in pupil outcomes from the effects of other contemporary changes. When
we examine those parts of the interview data which comment on the effects
on learning, however, replies often described the effects of resource
choices in a language which only indirectly represents changes in the
experiences of pupils. This was particularly notable for governors, less so
for head teachers and senior staff with teachers best at giving accounts
which are close to classroom practice. The key issue here is not the
language itself but the evidence base underlying the replies and which,
therefore, underpins the evaluation of the impact of resource choices.

We do not dismiss the value of those replies which refer indirectly to
benefits. A comment such as 'rapid response in producing high quality
learning materials' gives a sense of positive support for the core activity
of schools. This type of reply may also be adequate for its purpose: while
it is not a statement about what pupils do, it conveys a message which
most listeners would understand. In other words, there may be a common-
sense interpretation of the statement which means we understand its
consequences in the classroom. These replies may, therefore, be based
upon a good evidence base about needs in the classroom but that evidence
base is not explicit in the reply. It would be unwise too hastily to dismiss
such an interpretation.

On the other hand, replies such as this raise the possibility that some
decision-makers may in fact *be* too detached from the core activity of a
school. They may not be expressing the impact of their decisions in a
language of pupil effect because their evidence base is too weak. If that
were the case, decisions on resources may be ill-informed and, as a result,
inappropriate to educational needs and priorities.

There is no direct way by which these replies can be distinguished; we
cannot take a look inside the heads of those we interviewed! However, we
may be able to use other sources of information as a way of assessing the
evidence base underlying resource decisions – in this project and more
generally. We develop this argument in the next section as it has implications for schools as organisations.

Schools as cost-effective organisations

There are several sources of evidence which suggest that the three case study schools in this study approximate to being cost-effective, by which we mean they are using their responsibilities over resources (costs) in ways that are educationally successful (effective).

Interview and survey data from governors, head teachers, senior staff, teaching and support staff, parents and pupils, show a degree of consistency of opinion that we would be unwise to ignore. From their separate and collective views, the message we received was that decisions on resource priorities are largely consistent with their own assessment of needs. There would be cause for concern, for example, if the views of the head teacher and senior staff differed significantly from others. What we have, instead, are responses from a range of interests that point to agreement about priorities on resource allocation which suggest that these accord with their own assessment of need. While they may all be mistaken, we would be unwise to set aside these judgements too readily, all the more as we could not identify any compelling factors to support a different view.

These shared assessments of priorities suggest that these are schools where there is a good evidence base informing decisions, a finding which is consistent with other attributes of the schools as cost-effective organisations. The structures and processes of decision making at Broome, Skelton and Whittaker, for example, support the internal delegation of resource management. The interviews and observation notes show departments engaged in decisions on resources with heads of department sharing the process with colleagues. This internal delegation is accompanied by a dialogue of accountability with senior staff which contributes to the quality of debate informing decisions. These dialogues within departments and between teachers and senior staff are strengthened by access to information on pupil and student performance. In the relationship between teachers and senior staff, the latter have access to information on pupil and student learning which is independent of the teachers. This includes information not only from tests and formal examinations but from their review of the written work of pupils and students. Over time, we would expect these data to be enhanced further by information from the appraisal of teachers.

By contrast, our analysis does point to the dialogue with governors still being weak, not least because of their dependence on the education professionals for information. With the exception of formal examination results, there was no obvious source of independent information about the performance of the school. In obtaining information about each school and its needs, therefore, the head teacher is a particularly significant source. In the case of the three schools, we would not wish to misrepresent this situation. These were schools where the head teachers were concerned with encouraging their governors to be challenging in their dialogue with them and other staff, and each had governors who were able to engage in some of the forms of accountability we discussed in an earlier section of this chapter. The quality of several of the governors also suggested that if the schools were not well served by the head teacher, they were of a calibre that would have been aware of the problem. Whether they would have done anything to rectify such a problem, however, is unknown and leads us to consider a general issue arising from this limited dialogue.

Insofar as we have been able to judge, the three case study schools are good schools with good Heads. These Heads are pivotal in ensuring that their schools are developing as cost-effective organisations which have a number of the attributes we would expect them to have. Each Head plays a central role in ensuring that the evidence base on learning informs judgements on resource priorities. Their importance begs the question of what would occur if their successors were less effective in supporting the attributes of the cost-effective school. Are schools dependent upon their head teachers for their success? If so, the outlook is a matter for concern. Greater autonomy makes additional demands on head teachers, and reason suggests that we cannot expect all of them to be so good that their leadership will ensure that schools develop and improve in the demanding environment of the late 1990s. Indeed, we would expect the opposite with too many head teachers struggling to manage multiple demands in schools already preparing pupils for the next millennium.

The school system faces a dilemma. Delegation of resource management is welcomed by schools and it provides opportunities for improvement which would not otherwise be available. However, it also places additional demands on head teachers who currently have access to less support from outside bodies like LEAs than hitherto. Moreover, the evidence from our exemplars of good practice suggests that governors may not always be able to contribute sufficiently to a dialogue of accountability to ensure good quality assurance. In this, as in the quasi-market aspects of LMS and GMS, do we have a system where good head teachers can benefit from the opportunities offered to them but their weaker colleagues fail to do so? This concern together with the evidence of success in managing resources for school improvement informs the discussion in our final chapter.

Chapter 9

Sustaining improvement

We began this book by emphasising the importance of resources as the means by which we transform hopes and aspirations for children's education into daily experiences of teaching and learning. The delegation to schools of responsibility for the management of those resources is viewed by the government as a key element in its 'overall policy to improve the quality of teaching and learning in schools' (DES, 1988) and it has been the purpose of this book to describe, analyse and explain the attributes of good practice in that delegation. It has done so on the basis of practice in 18 secondary schools identified for us by HMI as likely examples of good practice. Good practice should not be confused with the ideal. We do not suggest, and no more would those whom we met in the schools, that these schools cannot improve or develop the way they use their responsibilities. They do, however, provide examples which assist our understanding of resource management and from which we can learn. In this chapter, our intention is to consider what can be learnt from these schools in a discussion which is organised around those organisational attributes we believe must be added to effective schools to make them cost-effective.

AUDIT, COSTS AND OPTIONS

The accounts of delegation in the 15 schools and the three case study schools show the many ways in which all 18 have used their delegated powers, whether under local management or grant maintained status. Developments have occurred in relation to teaching and support staff, school administration, the environment, the use of space and expenditure on curriculum materials. In responding to this new environment, we draw particular attention to the use made of external support. We need not repeat the examples cited earlier but observe the enthusiasm with which schools have used their powers to direct resources into those areas which they had identified as priorities.

These changes reflect a readiness to employ and deploy people and physical resources in ways that differ from previous practice in the schools. When changes have implications for the working practices of existing staff, these schools were likely to recognise their professional development needs, thereby making real change more likely. In these ways, schools exhibited some of the features of what we describe as *radical audit*. There is, however, scope for further change, and shared experience from the practice of delegation may lead in that direction. The study by Mortimore and Mortimore with Thomas (1994) illustrates the already growing diversity of practice in the employment of staff and the commentary on the teaching profession prepared by Barber and Brighouse (1992) indicates the scope for the development of new 'associate teacher' roles in schools.

> National initiatives reviewing the role of the teacher could lead to fitness-for-purpose replacing traditional practice as the principle underlying decisions on resource priorities.

With better information on *costs*, reviews of role can also be guided by information on costs as well as effectiveness. In several schools, the linkage of purpose and priorities with resource choices was evident in the School Development Plan as a published document. Plans showed the developments likely to absorb staff effort but these resources were rarely expressed in financial terms. Curriculum developments, for example, were normally described in terms of what needed to be done rather than the financial equivalent of the time of teachers. This is not inappropriate in its emphasis on educational tasks but it may also be a consequence of how existing financial information is presented, whereby financial information systems are not being used to generate data in these formats.

In Chapter 3 (Figure 3.2), we showed a formal means for attempting to identify the costs, benefits and forgone opportunities of proposed changes. We would not necessarily expect many schools to prepare such a summary of the *options* they are considering but means are available for decision-makers having better information to inform their judgements. Evidence we collected on financial information in these schools, and particularly from the case studies, showed them using their existing systems well, in the sense that they had up to date, reliable information managed by staff well able to draw out necessary data as required. As with most other schools, however, the form of the financial information was seldom analysed to departments and other cost centres where expenditure occurs. Instead, the schools tended to work with a diversity of resource information, including traditional school-level financial information, limited departmental cost-centre data for expenditure on learning materials and professional development, as well as curriculum analyses showing the disposition of staff to departments and subjects.

It may be that this diversity of data is sufficient for the whole task of audit, costing and review of options, but we have our doubts. The approach we outlined in Chapter 3 enables the costs of different resources to be compared using a common unit of account – money – and options considered against these costs. The failure of schools to make general use of the cost-centring potential of existing financial information may indicate that it has little to offer them in terms of better information. It may be, however, that schools and LEAs are so familiar with the traditional format of budgets and expenditure that an alternative is seen as an unwelcome change. For locally managed schools, it is an area where LEAs could stimulate change by reviewing their own accounting and reporting practices so that schools are encouraged to modify their approach and show spending cost centred in the school.

> LEAs can lead change in the presentation of financial information with spending shown by cost centres and the costs of new developments linked to assessment of benefit.

Greater innovation in the presentation of financial information, so that costs are more clearly linked to options being considered, is also a way of opening the decision process to others. If management information can be presented so that it shows options, more people can engage in a discussion about priorities and choice. Clearer presentation of these data is a way of assisting schools in a review of the cost-effectiveness of their current deployment of staff. More important, however, is the need for training programmes for head teachers to give attention to issues of fitness-for-purpose – from which more cost-effective use of staff is more likely to follow. The area is a clear example of the importance of training, a general issue recognised by the OECD (1994) synthesis report on delegation schemes.

DELEGATION, DIALOGUE AND DETACHMENT

The schools we visited were using their authority over resources in ways which were clearly linked to their overall aims, purposes and priorities. The themes of purposeful educational leadership and collegiate planning reported in the literature on school effectiveness are also apparent in this study of resource management.

The importance of the process underlying the preparation of the plan was evident. In many schools, those whom we interviewed spoke of development planning when they gave accounts of how the school made decisions on the use of resources. This applied to priorities for the whole school and within departments, where *internal delegation* meant departments and faculties had responsibility for resources and priorities in their own areas. Overall, the planning process recognised the primacy of the curriculum: staffing issues, programmes of improvement to premises and priorities for learning materials typically were led by the requirements of the National Curriculum and assessment. In effect, the plans and the planning process were concerned with the educational needs of the schools. They were also used by some head teachers as a means of securing participation by others in agreeing priorities and, subsequently, using the agreed plan as a means of maintaining awareness of those priorities.

The role of development planning as a means of participatory management illustrates its place in the *dialogue of accountability* in these schools. In all 18 the role of the head teacher in this dialogue was pivotal. Above all others, it was the head teacher who gave shape and direction to developments, maintaining a focus upon the growth of the school as an educational enterprise. The head teacher also plays an important role in developing the governing body, acting as its adviser, mentor and guide. Governors, who undertake this public service on a voluntary basis, have had to come to terms with major changes in their role and are entitled to advice and guidance. What we observed in the best of these relationships was advice from head teachers which did not lead the governing body to a single pre-determined decision but enabled individual governors to bring their own background knowledge and experience to the issues being discussed. It meant that governing bodies gave due weight to professional advice without being 'rubber stamps'. We do, nonetheless, express concern about the access of governors to information which is independent of the head teacher and other staff in the schools. Such concern must be all the greater in schools where, unlike these, head teachers may be less disposed to support the development of their governing body.

The head teacher also leads the staff and this is done in distinctive ways. The circumstances of the three case study schools are illustrative of head teachers seeking to encourage the development of their staff, the nature and extent of staff participation differing because of the local context and the duration of the head teacher in post. At Skelton, for example, a head teacher of long standing had been able to extend professional participation to resource management issues quite quickly. It is at Skelton that we distinguish between the head teacher as an *initiator* of many policies but also acting as a *supporter* or sponsor of proposals made by others. At Broome, staff were still dependent upon the head teacher as the *initiator*, although others were now developing in confidence and capacity. At Whittaker, where the head teacher had been in post for less than one year, there remained much work to be done to encourage staff to recognise the need to respond more actively and be less passive recipients of change. The dialogue characterising these different forms of participation was informed by independent evidence on the quality of learning in the schools. Unlike the governors, the head teachers had direct access to the work of pupils and students, giving them a stronger evidence base for determining needs and priorities. As in the support given to governors, much depends upon how head teachers interpret their role and exercise their responsibilities. The emphasis on autonomy in locally managed and grant maintained schools works well with good head teachers but they rely heavily upon the abilities of one person.

Interview and survey evidence from teachers, parents, pupils and students in our three case study schools suggest that the head teachers and other decision-makers were broadly correct in their assessment of needs and priorities. In this sense they have been successful in reducing the information problems associated with the *detachment of management*. More generally, the surveys of pupils, student and parent opinion provide distinctive voices which illuminate issues differently from those of governors, head teacher and other staff.

> There is a need for more regular and systematic sampling of the views of parents, pupils and students. It is an activity which could be managed by LEAs, whose role in a delegated system should include a greater focus on representing client interests.

Information such as this has the added benefit of being *independent* of the education professionals. It is pupils and students who experience classroom practice most directly and for whom it is a daily experience. Their responses to our attitude statements and the additional comments they provided show them making sensible and realistic assessments of their daily school experiences. Through surveys, school management could obtain regular feedback on the range of their provision in the school. This is all the more important in view of the detachment of management, not least governors, from the core activity of schools and their resulting difficulty in assessing the impact on learning of resource choices. Our study notes a tendency for effects to be expressed in terms of tangible changes, such as additional reprographic facilities or more computers. These are important statements of effect, reporting what are seen as substantive changes as a result of delegated management, but it is important, nonetheless, to recognise that they are not direct statements of change in learning. Assessing the impact of delegation in terms of *measured* effect on learning is unlikely but seeking to get closer to the classroom effects is important if we are to avoid being preoccupied by second-order factors – which may be misleading.

These 18 secondary schools exhibit the changes brought about by the reforms of LMS and GMS. They have visibly changed in appearance and in how they set about some of the things that they do. They have harnessed the flexibility of resource management to their purposes and priorities as educational institutions. In doing so perhaps they exhibit, above all, the importance of continuity as well as change in the management of education. Continuity is embodied in a purposeful leadership which gives primacy to the educational needs of students at their schools. Change is found at every turn, the same leadership taking advantage of its new powers to strengthen the quality of teaching and learning in its schools.

CONCLUSION: CHOICE, DIVERSITY AND IMPROVEMENT

The schools we have had the opportunity to study demonstrate the potential and benefits of delegating responsibilities for resource management to the school site. They also show the task is a challenging one, demanding judgements in conditions of uncertainty which belie management nostrums which sometimes refer too easily to setting objectives, allocating resources and evaluating outcomes. In the uncertainty endemic to school management we have drawn attention to the detachment of management from the core activity of schools and asked whether management in the schools we have studied has overcome that detachment sufficiently to be informed about educational needs. Some of the interview data give cause for doubt, our study showing the effects of resource choices on pupils being expressed in a language of tangible changes more than a language of altered classroom practice. Other parts of the interview and survey data show sufficient agreement on priorities to suggest that the judgements and decisions of management correspond with those of others in the schools. That this should be so says much for the role and judgement of the head teachers in these schools, whose access to a range and quality of information makes them pre-eminent in decision making. It is this pre-eminence that provides us with the basis for our closing argument because existing forms of delegated management appear to depend too much on the capacities of one person in each school.

A dialogue of accountability provides the means by which judgements about educational needs are tested and priorities in the allocation of resources decided. The quality of that dialogue depends too much upon the head teacher. Even in the three case study schools where the head teachers were supporting the development of the governing body, the information which underpins the decisions of governors normally comes from the head teacher. Providing governors with a source of information independent of the head teacher and teachers in their school is a necessary condition for enabling their greater participation in the dialogue of accountability. We believe that the LEA is the appropriate agency for undertaking such a task, providing schools with information about their own performance and those of other schools. Examination data and survey data on parent, pupil and student attitudes to their schools provide a better evidence base for managers and can contribute to a wider perspective on the range of school activities. We have also argued that LEAs should develop better management information systems in order to stimulate greater creativity in schools in the employment and deployment of staff. These are not developments that should be left to chance but should be required by changes in the legal duties of LEAs so that their obligations to parents, pupils and students as clients are emphasised. It is a responsibility which should extend to grant maintained schools which could retain their existing level of financial and staffing responsibilities but whose performance in providing a service would become a matter for reporting by a client-centred LEA. They are changes which would add another voice to the dialogue of accountability, requiring LEAs to work with governors and staff in judging whether needs are being properly assessed and resources allocated in accordance with priorities. This can assist in the improvement of delegated management by taking account of the level of professional expertise in specific schools, providing support as necessary.

Our interview and survey data from Broome, Skelton and Whittaker point to three schools that have the attributes and achievements of cost-effective schools. The more limited data from the 15 other schools make such a judgement difficult, although they were all creative and positive in their exercise of resource management. Choice and diversity in the management of resources characterise all these schools. The challenge to government is to build upon the best of delegated management by recognising some of the problems and weaknesses in its existing schemes so that delegated management in all schools can contribute to and sustain educational improvement.

Appendix
Profiles of the schools

The first field work phase of the project focused on visits to 18 secondary schools. Subsequently three were chosen for case study. These were all identified as institutions representing circumstances where the new responsibilities and context for school management are being used to enhance educational effectiveness. Data thus gathered have enabled the project to identify specific examples of good practice in education resource management, some key trends in the use of resources and significant issues in school decision making concerning resources.

While the choice of schools was based on HMI recommendation, the sample does represent a cross-section of types of secondary school. Two are inner-city schools with high ethnic minority intakes. Four schools are situated in industrial suburbs with predominantly white working class intake. Four are in middle class suburbs and the remainder are situated in county town or rural environments. The spread of the size of school is wide, the smallest number on roll being 607 and the largest 1,765. The majority of schools are 11–18 age range including a sixth form although three of those have intakes from the ages of 12, 13 and 14 respectively. Four of the schools are 11–16 age range. Only one of the schools studied has a selective intake and two are single sex.

Thirteen schools are locally managed and maintained by the LEA. Five of these had capital projects in progress. Five schools has transferred from local authority control and become grant maintained. All of these had benefited from or were applying for capital grants in the coming year. Two schools enjoyed substantial distinctive funding from foundation trusts.

School 1 is an 11–18 inner-city, split-site comprehensive school with 95 per cent ethnic minority intake. It has been locally managed since April 1990 and a local management pilot school since 1989. The school is popular and full to its standard number with rising numbers in the sixth form.

School 2 (Broome School) is an inner-city comprehensive school with an 11–16 age group. The number on roll is 607 and expected to rise in the coming years. The school recruits from a wide area and comprises 85 per cent ethnic minorities, largely Asian. The school has been locally managed since April 1990.

School 3 is an 11–18 comprehensive school serving a rural community. The number on roll has been increasing and now stands at 1,215. In anticipation of this trend continuing the school is presently being extended by the local authority at a cost of £2.75m. The school has been locally managed since April 1990.

School 4 is a large 11–18 comprehensive school serving the suburban population of a county town. The number on roll is 1,765 and expected to rise in future years, with 332 pupils in the sixth form. A former grammar school, the school has a reputation for good academic results, and attracts a white middle class intake. Until recently the school was on a split site but has recently reorganised onto one campus with a local authority funded capital building programme, which the school has enhanced with funds from a Governors' Foundation Fund. This fund also aids the school with some maintainence costs. The school benefits financially from substantial lettings from a manor house which forms part of the school site. The school has been involved as a local management pilot school since 1983 and is now locally managed.

School 5 is an 11–16 urban comprehensive school with a predominantly white working class intake. The school has increased in popularity over recent years, despite a downward demographic trend in the area, and is oversubscribed with a number on roll of 765. Having been a pilot school, it became fully locally managed on April 1990. Previously a dual-use site in collaboration with the LEA, the school now manages its own lettings which generate extra funds.

School 6 is an 11–16 comprehensive school situated in industrial city suburbs with a white working class intake; 25 per cent of the pupils are registered for free school meals. The school has been increasing in popularity since 1990 and has 775 on roll with 830 projected for September 1993. A local management pilot school since 1989, the school has been locally managed since April 1990 and has dual use of the school site with the LEA for evening adult classes and a community leisure centre. This has resulted in the school receiving some matched funding from the Local Education Authority for the improvement of premises.

School 7 is an 11–18 comprehensive community school serving a rural community bordering a county town. The number on roll is 922 with an increase up to 1,000 projected by September 1995. The school is increasing in popularity and now offers its own transport for pupils travelling from the county town. There are 120 pupils in the sixth form which operates as a co-operative with nearby schools. The school is a thriving adult educa-tion and community centre out of school hours which is presently managed in collaboration with the LEA. The school is locally managed and is presently reorganising onto one campus from a split site as a capital building project funded by the LEA.

School 8 is a suburban comprehensive which has recently changed intake from a 12–18 to 11–18 age group. The school is oversubscribed with a standard number of 210. There are 250 pupils in the sixth form. Locally managed since 1990, the school buildings were declared unsafe due to structural faults as a result of which the school has a five-year £6m building programme in progress funded by the LEA. The school is in a particularly competitive environment with independent and selective schools within close proximity in neighbouring authorities.

School 9 is a 13–18 boys' comprehensive school. From a situation of falling rolls the school now has 910 pupils, with increasing numbers projected in the coming years, and 210 pupils in the sixth form. A former city grammar school, it continues to enjoy the benefits of a Governors' Foundation Fund for capital and maintenance moneys. The school has been a local manage-ment pilot school since 1988, locally managed since 1990 and grant maintained since January 1992.

School 10 is an 11–18 comprehensive community college serving a large rural population. It has 1,070 pupils with 150 in the sixth form. Having been a local management pilot school, the school is now locally managed.

School 11 (Skelton High School) is an 11–16 suburban comprehensive school with 1,195 pupils on roll. The school is popular with local parents and its total student number is rising despite a downward demographic trend in the area. The school has been locally managed since April 1991.

School 12 is a 14–18 comprehensive community college serving a county town. The number on roll is 787 with a projected rising trend to 828 in 1996. The school has been locally managed since April 1990 and has a delegated budget from the LEA for community education.

School 13 is a selective 11–18 girls' school situated in a city suburb. Less than 1 per cent of the pupils have free meals and about 6 per cent are from minority ethnic groups. The number on roll is 707 with 203 in the sixth form. The school gained grant maintained status in April 1992.

School 14 is an 11–18 comprehensive school serving a rural community. Numbers on roll are projected to increase and currently stand at 823. There are 77 students in the sixth form which is part of a local consortium. The school has been locally managed since April 1990.

School 15 (Whittaker School) is a 12–18 comprehensive school in a semirural environment. Locally managed since April 1990, the school became grant maintained on 1 April 1993. The school is oversubscribed with a number on roll of 1,111 and 170 students in the sixth form.

School 16 is an 11–18 county town comprehensive school. It is presently oversubscribed and has an extension building programme near to completion, funded by the LEA. It is planned to expand the sixth form. Part of a local management pilot scheme since 1986, the school has been locally managed since 1992 and became grant maintained in January 1993.

School 17 is an 11–18 Roman Catholic, voluntary aided, urban comprehensive school on a split site. It traditionally takes pupils from two Local Education Authorities in the surrounding conurbation. The school is oversubscribed with 1,325 on roll and 230 in the sixth form. It has been locally managed since 1989 and became grant maintained in September 1992.

School 18 is an 11–18 mixed comprehensive school serving a diverse population from the county town in which it is situated and the surrounding areas. It has been grant maintained since April 1992. The number on roll is rising but presently stands at 1,094 with 165 students in the sixth form.

References

Arnott, M.A., Bullock, A.D. and Thomas, H.R. (1992) *The Impact of Local Management on Schools. A Source Book. The First Report of the 'Impact' Project*, 109 pp. University of Birmingham, School of Education.

Barber, M. and Brighouse, T. (1992) *Partners in Change. Enhancing the Teaching Profession*, London: IPPR.

Behrman, J.R. (1993) *Measuring the Cost-effectiveness of Schooling Policies: Revisiting Issues of Methodology*, presented at the International Symposium on the Economics of Education, British Council, 18–21 May.

Bullock, A.D. and Thomas, H. (1994) *The Impact of Local Management on Schools: Final Report*, 163 pp., University of Birmingham, School of Education.

Bullock, A.D. and Thomas, H. (1996) *Schools at the Centre?*, London: Routledge.

Burridge, E. and Ribbins, P. (1994) 'Promoting improvement in schools: aspects of quality in Birmingham'. In Ribbins, P. and Burridge, E. (eds) *Improving Education. Promoting Quality in Schools*, London: Cassell.

Bush, T. *et al.* (1993) *Managing Autonomous Schools: The Grant Maintained Experience*, London: Chapman.

Caines, Sir J. (1992) 'Improving education through better management: a view from the DES'. In Simkins, T., Ellison, L. and Garrett, V. (eds) *Implementing Educational Reform. The Early Lessons*, Harlow: Longman for BEMAS.

Caldwell, B.J. (1994) 'Leading the transformation of Australia's schools', *Educational Management and Administration* 22(2): 76–84.

Caldwell, B.J. and Spinks, J.M. (1988) *The Self-Managing School*, Lewes: The Falmer Press.

Cheng, Y.C. (1993) 'The theory and characteristics of school-based management', *International Journal of Educational Management* 7(6): 6–7.

Chubb, J.E. and Moe, T.M. (1990) *Politics, Markets and America's Schools*, Washington, DC: Brookings Institution.

Coopers and Lybrand (1988) *Local Management of Schools: A Report to the Department of Education and Science*, London: DES.

Dalin, P. (1989) 'Reconceptualising the school improvement process: a review of the British literature'. In Reynolds, D., Creemers, B.P.M. and Peters, T. (eds) *School Effectiveness and Improvement*, School of Education, University of Wales College of Cardiff and Groningen: RION Institute for Educational Research.

Davies, B. and Hentshke, G. (1994) 'School autonomy: myth or reality – developing an analytical taxonomy', *Educational Management and Administration* 22(2): 96–103.

DES (1987) *Financial Delegation to Schools: Consultation Paper*, London: DES.

DES (1988) *Education Reform Act: Local Management of Schools*, Circular 7/88, London: DES.

DES (1989) *Planning for School Development I: Advice to Governors, Headteachers and Teachers*, London: DES.

DES (1990) *Planning for School Development II*, London: DES.

DFE (1992) *The Implementation of Local Management of Schools: A Report by HM Inspectorate*, London: HMSO.

DFE (1993) *Effective Management in Schools: A Report from the School Management Task Force Professional Working Party*, London: HMSO.

DFE/WO (1992) *Choice and Diversity*, Cmd 2021, London: HMSO.

Downes, P. (ed.) (1988) *Local Financial Management in Schools*, Oxford: Blackwell.

Fullan, M. (1992) *What's Worth Fighting for in Headship*, Milton Keynes: The Open University Press.

Fullan, M. and Hargreaves, A. (1992) *What's Worth Fighting for in Your School*, Milton Keynes: The Open University Press.

Hanushek, E.A. (1979) 'Conceptual and empirical issues in the estimation of production functions', *Journal of Human Resources* 14(3): 351–87.

Hargreaves, D. and Hopkins, D. (1991) *The Empowered School*, London: Cassell.

Hewlett, J. (1988) 'Local financial management: a case study of Alderbrook School, Solihull', *School Organisation* 8(2): 147–57.

HMI (1977) *Ten Good Schools: A Secondary School Enquiry*, London: HMSO.

HMI (1992) *Non-Teaching Staff in Schools. A Review by HMI*, London: HMSO.

Hopkins, D. and Ainscow, M. (1993) 'Making sense of school improvement: an interim account of the "Improving the Quality of Education for All" Project', *Cambridge Journal of Education* 23(3): 287–304.

Humphrey, C. and Thomas, H. (1985) 'Giving schools the money', *Education* 165(19): 419–20.

Kirkpatrick, G. (1988) 'Local financial management: case study of a junior school', *School Organisation* 8(2): 155–170.

Knight, B. (1993) 'Delegated financial management and school effectiveness'. In Dimmock, C. (ed.) *School-Based Management and School Effectiveness*, London: Routledge.

Koppich, J.E. and Guthrie, J.W. (1993) 'Examining contemporary education-reform efforts in the United States'. In Beare, H. and Boyd, W.L. (eds) *Restructuring Schools. An International Perspective on the Movement to Transform the Control and Performance of Schools*, London: The Falmer Press.

Levacic, R. (1992) 'Local management of schools: aims, scope and impact', *Educational Management and Administration* 20(1): 16–29.

Levacic, R. and Glover, D. (1994) *Ofsted Assessment of Schools' Efficiency*, Milton Keynes: Centre for Educational Policy and Management, Open University.

Levin, H.M. (1976) 'Concepts of economic efficiency and educational production'. In Froomkin, J.T. *et al.* (eds) *Education as an Industry*, NBER, Cambridge, MA.: Ballinger.

Lieberman, M. (1993) *Public Education. An Autopsy*, Cambridge, MA: Harvard University Press.

Macpherson, R.J.S. (1993) 'The reconstruction of New Zealand education: a case of "high politics" reform?'. In Beare, H. and Boyd, W.L. (eds) *Restructuring Schools. An International Perspective on the Movement to Transform the Control and Performance of Schools*, London: The Falmer Press.

Marland, M. (1991) 'Governing the school: the legal responsibilities for the curriculum'. Unpublished paper.

Marland, M. (1992) 'How to make use of the Acts'. In *The Times Educational Supplement*, 4 September, p. 19.

Marren, E. and Levacic, R. (1992) 'Implementing local management of schools: first year spending decisions'. In Simkins, T., Ellison, L. Garrett, (eds)*Implementing Educational Reform: The Early Lessons*, Harlow: Longman for BEMAS.

Mortimore, P. and Mortimore, J. with Thomas, H. (1994) *Managing Associate Staff: Innovation in Primary and Secondary Schools*, London: Chapman.

Mortimore, P., MacGilchrist, B. and Savage, J. (1995) *The Impact of School Development Plans in Primary Schools*, London: University of London Institute of Education.

Mortimore, P., Sammons, P., Stoll, L., Lewis, D. and Ecob, R. (1988) *School Matters. The Junior Years*, London: Open Books.

National Audit Office (1994) *Value for Money at Grant-Maintained Schools: A Review of Performance*, London: HMSO.

OECD (1994) *Effectiveness of Schooling and of Educational Resource Management*, DEELSA/ED(94) 17, Paris: OECD.

Ofsted (1993) *Grant Maintained Schools: A Report from the Office of Her Majesty's Chief Inspector of Schools*, London: HMSO.

Ofsted (1995) *The Annual Report of Her Majesty's Chief Inspector of Schools*, London: HMSO.

Reynolds, D., Sullivan, M. and Murgatroyd, S.J. (1987) *The Comprehensive Experiment*, Lewes: The Falmer Press.

Ribbins, P. and Burridge, E. (eds) (1994) *Improving Education. Promoting Quality in Schools*, London: Cassell.

Rutter, M., Maughan, B., Mortimore, P. and Ouston, J. (1979) *Fifteen Thousand Hours – Secondary Schools and their Effects on Children*, London: Open Books.

Scottish Office, The (1992a) *Using Ethos Indicators in Primary School Self-Evaluation. Taking Account of the Views of Pupils, Parents and Teachers*, HM Inspectors of Schools, Edinburgh: The Scottish Office Education Department.

Scottish Office, The (1992b) *Using Ethos Indicators in Secondary School Self-Evaluation. Taking Account of the Views of Pupils, Parents and Teachers*, HM Inspectors of Schools, Edinburgh: The Scottish Office Education Department.

Sharpe, F. (1994) 'Devolution – towards a research framework', *Educational Management and Administration* 22(2): 85–95.

Simkins, T. (1992) 'Policy, accountability and management: perspectives on the implementation of reform'. In Simkins, T., Ellison, L. and Garrett, V. (eds) *Implementing Educational Reform. The Early Lessons*, Harlow: Longman for BEMAS.

Simkins, T., Ellison, L. and Garrett, V. (eds) (1992) *Implementing Educational Reform. The Early Lessons*, Harlow: Longman for BEMAS.

Southworth, G. (1994) 'The learning school'. In Ribbins, P. and Burridge, E. (eds) *Improving Education. Promoting Quality in Schools*, London: Cassell.

Thomas, H. (1987) 'Efficiency and opportunity in school finance autonomy'. In Thomas, H. and Simkins, T. (eds) *Economics and the Management of Education: Emerging Themes*, Lewes: The Falmer Press.

Thomas, H. (1990) *Education Costs and Performance. A Cost-effectiveness Analysis*, London: Cassell.

Thomas, H. (1994) 'Markets, collectivities and management', *Oxford Review of Education* 20(1): 41–56.

Thomas, H. with Kirkpatrick, G and Nicholson, E. (1989) *Financial Delegation and the Local Management of Schools: Preparing for Practice*, London: Cassell.

Thomas, H. and Martin, J. (1994) *The Effectiveness of Schooling and Education Resource Management: A Report for DFE/OECD*, University of Birmingham, School of Education.

Windham, D.M. and Chapman, D.W. (1990) *The Evaluation of Educational Efficiency: Constraints, Issues and Policies*, Greenwich, CT, JAI Press.

Index

arrangements for 144; pay,
conditions and 63–4; preparation of
suitable programmes 21; support
for 122
PTAs (Parent–Teacher Associations)
61, 72, 76, 82, 165
PTR (Pupil–Teacher Ratio) 60, 93
punctuality 105
punishment 16
pupils: assessments 7; behaviour 95;
comments by 170–1; concern to
improve awareness of and concern
for environment 70; curriculum
meets needs and preferences 60–1;
intake 93, 111; librarians 97;
motivation and attitude 170;
practical assistance for 80; premises
refurbishment appreciated by 140;
records 68, 71; reorganisation
greeted with approval by 139;
reporting systems 69; satisfaction
levels 138–9; statements 143; survey
data from 92; views 40–1

quality 10, 12, 17, 176; assessments of
44; assurance 180; dangers of
complacency about 43; educational
experiences 26; effect of LMS and
GMS on 27; enhancing 111;
environment 72, 95; feedback on 8;
governors 180; Heads must
emphasise 15; human resources
151; improvement projects 87;
management 115; no guarantee of
32; services 25; staff 148; teachers
complacent about 39; teaching 27,
92; see also quality of learning
quality of learning 30, 32, 45, 69, 136,
166; assessment of 39; consequence
of delegation for 26; enhanced
effectiveness in 27; high 79;
information on 43, 175; resources
needed to improve 92
quantitative techniques 23

radical audit 36, 42, 91, 135, 155, 171,
182
reading: assessment 111; attitudes to
95; learning 96; opportunity to help
improve skills 97
recording effectiveness of procedures
for 32
Records of Achievement 62, 90, 102; co-

ordinator for 68
recruitment 119
redundancy 17
refurbishment 55, 88, 158; building
158; classrooms 164; cloakroom
areas 140; funded from school
budget 139; general 99–101; public
areas 72; rolling programmes 89,
139; science facilities 70; teaching
rooms 72, 79–80; technology suites
97–9
repair(s) 70; minor 85; poor state of 141
reprographics 65, 75; budget for 78;
facilities 80; no bottleneck in 119,
170; part-time technicians 93;
support 169
resources 49–92; deployment of 8;
improvement and 3–9
resources management 49–92, 145–54;
and cost- effectiveness 22–4; good
practice 5; reforming 10–19; wide
range of voices and opinions 6
reward 16, 118
Reynolds, D. 29
Ribbins, P. 29
Rutter, M. 29

salaries 63–4, 132; bill reduced by
appointment of younger staff 122;
costs 42; discretion over 118
Savage, J. 37
school budget 20
School Development Groups 103, 104,
108
School Development Plans 34, 44,
103–4, 128–9, 146–7; audit stage 92;
budget statement contained in 135;
departmental 91, 142, 153;
governors responsible for
approving 30; issues which needed
to be tackled 87; items raised at
Academic Board 110; no
recollection of 152; one of the
targets 81; place of 51; preparation
27, 52, 63, 131, 156; projects 106;
regarded as vital 151; resource
implications 132, 150, 182; seminar
which audited/reviewed work on
56
school environment: caring 167;
improving 139–41; learning 95, 96,
157; secure, potential threat to 147;
statements on 124–5; teaching 157;